• HBJ READING PROGRAM •

WINDMILLS

 LAUREATE EDITION

LEVEL 7

Bernice E. Cullinan
Roger C. Farr
W. Dorsey Hammond
Nancy L. Roser
Dorothy S. Strickland

HBJ **HARCOURT BRACE JOVANOVICH, PUBLISHERS**
Orlando   San Diego   Chicago   Dallas

Acknowledgments

For permission to reprint copyrighted material, grateful acknowledgment is made to the following sources:

Curtis Brown, Ltd.: "Girls Can, Too" from *Girls Can, Too* by Lee Bennett Hopkins. Copyright © 1972 by Lee Bennett Hopkins. Published by Franklin Watts, Inc. Adapted from the second half of "The Galumpagalooses" by Eloise Jarvis McGraw. Copyright © 1983 by Eloise Jarvis McGraw. Originally published in *Cricket* Magazine.

Childrens Press: Adapted from *Sally Ride, Astronaut: An American First* by June Behrens. Copyright © 1984 by Regensteiner Publishing Enterprises, Inc.

Judith H. Ciardi: "How to Tell the Top of a Hill" from *The Reason for the Pelican* by John Ciardi. Copyright 1959 by John Ciardi.

Coward, McCann & Geoghegan, Inc.: Adapted from *Nate the Great and the Missing Key* by Marjorie Weinman Sharmat. Text copyright © 1981 by Marjorie Weinman Sharmat.

E. P. Dutton, a division of NAL Penguin Inc.: Adapted from *My Friend Jacob* by Lucille Clifton, illustrated by Thomas DiGrazia. Text copyright © 1980 by Lucille Clifton; illustrations copyright © 1980 by Thomas DiGrazia. Adapted from *The Balancing Girl* by Berniece Rabe, pictures by Lillian Hoban. Text copyright © 1981 by Berniece Rabe; illustrations copyright © 1981 by Lillian Hoban.

Greenwillow Books, a division of William Morrow & Company, Inc.: "Whistling" from *Rainy Rainy Saturday* by Jack Prelutsky. Text copyright © 1980 by Jack Prelutsky.

Harper & Row, Publishers, Inc.: "Rudolph is Tired of the City" from *Bronzeville Boys and Girls* by Gwendolyn Brooks. Copyright © 1956 by Gwendolyn Brooks. "The Question" from *Dogs & Dragons, Trees & Dreams* by Karla Kuskin. Copyright © 1958 by Karla Kuskin. Poem No. 19 from *Any Me I Want to Be* by Karla Kuskin. Copyright © 1972 by Karla Kuskin. Complete text, abridged and adapted, and illustrations from *The Cloud*, written and illustrated by Deborah Kogan Ray. Copyright © 1984 by Deborah Kogan Ray.

Highlights for Children, Inc., Columbus, OH: "City Grandfather, Country Grandfather" by Robert Hasselblad and adapted from "Thanks to Mary" by Ann Bixby Herold in *Highlights for Children*, February 1985. Copyright © 1985 by Highlights for Children, Inc.

Gina Maccoby Literary Agency: "Brother" from *Hello and Good-by* by Mary Ann Hoberman. Copyright © 1959, renewed 1987 by Mary Ann Hoberman. Published by Little, Brown and Company.

McIntosh and Otis, Inc.: "The Goat Who Couldn't Sneeze" from *The Burro Benedicto and Other Folktales and Legends of Mexico* by Philip D. Jordan. Text copyright © 1960 by Philip D. Jordan.

Modern Curriculum Press, Inc.: Adapted from *The Mystery of Sara Beth* by Polly Putnam. Copyright © 1981 by Polly Putnam Mathews.

Pantheon Books, a division of Random House, Inc.: Adapted from *Big Boss! Little Boss!* (Titled: "Little Boss") by Barbara Bottner. Copyright © 1978 by Barbara Bottner. Adapted from *Backyard Basketball Superstar* by Monica Klein. Copyright © 1981 by Monica Klein.

Marian Reiner, on behalf of Kathleen Fraser: "Broom Balancing" from *Stilts, Somersaults and Headstands* by Kathleen Fraser. Copyright © 1968 by Kathleen Fraser. Published by Atheneum Publishers, Inc.

Viking Penguin Inc.: From *Talking Without Words*, written and illustrated by Marie Hall Ets. Copyright © 1968 by Marie Hall Ets. Adapted from *Today Was a Terrible Day* by Patricia Reilly Giff. Copyright © 1980 by Patricia Reilly Giff.

Franklin Watts, Inc.: From *Jasper and the Hero Business* by Betty Horvath. Text copyright © 1977 by Franklin Watts, Inc.

Albert Whitman & Company: From *My Grandpa Retired Today* by Elaine Knox-Wagner. Text © 1982 by Elaine Knox-Wagner.

Photographs

Key: (1) - Left; (r) - Right; (c) - Center; (t) - Top; (b) - Bottom.

Page iii, H. Zefa/H. Armstrong Roberts; iv, David Muench; vi, HBJ Photo; vi, Ewing Galloway; vii, HBJ Photo/John Petrey; Page 2, Messerschmidt/Leo de Wys; 3, Shostal; 16, HBJ Photo; 17 (all), HBJ Photo; 18 (all), HBJ Photo; 19 (all), HBJ Photo; 20, HBJ Photo; 46, HBJ Photo; 47 (all), HBJ Photo/Lloyd Hryciw; 48, HBJ Photo/Lloyd Hryciw; 49 (all), HBJ Photo/Llyod Hryciw; 50, Photri, Inc.; 61, Shostal; 62, Galen Rowell/FPG; 63, Wheeler Pictures; 102, NASA from Photri, Inc.; 103, NASA; 104, Wide World Photos; 105, NASA; 106, NASA from Photri, Inc.; 110, Index/Stone International, Inc.; 112, Jon Eastcott and Yva Momatiuk/The Image Works; 113, Robert H. Galze/Artstreet; 127, Galen Rowell, FPG; 128, Ewing Galloway; 129 (1), Stan Ries/Leo de Wys; 129 (r), Richard Hutchings; 154, Camera photo, Venice; 155, Musee National d'Art Moderne/Art Resource; 156, Musee National d'Art Moderne/Art Resource; 157, National Gallery of Art; 158, National Gallery of Art; 191, Stan Ries/Leo de Wys; 192-193, HBJ Photo/John Petrey; 273, HBJ Photo/John Petrey.

Illustrators

Lynn Adams: 244–247; Michael Adams; 116–117, 226–230; Ray App: 66–74; Allen Atkinson: 196–204; Rowan Baines-Murphy: 90–100; Alex Bloch: 24–30; Shirley Breuel: 44–45, 180–181; Susan Brooks: 256–270; Dee Deloy: 76; Robert Jackson: 206–207; John Killigrew: 224–225; Larry Mikec: 6–12; Jerry Pinkney: 146–152; Tom Powers: 111, 114; Sally Schaedler: 52–58; Georgia Shola: 76–77; Dan Siculan: 160–170, 232–242, 248–254; Blanche Sims: 78–86; Samantha Smith: 142; Jozef Sumicrast: 216–222
Cover: Robert Rodriguez

Printed in the United States of America

ISBN 0-15-330008-6

Contents

Unit 1
Winding Roads 2

Unit 2
Mountaintops 62

Unit 3
Bridges

Unit 4
Patterns

Awards

The authors and illustrators of selections in this book have received the following awards either for their work in this book or for another of their works. The specific award is indicated under the medallion on the opening page of each award-winning selection.

The American Book Award
American Library Association Notable Children's Books
L. Frank Baum Award
Randolph Caldecott Honor Award
Lewis Carroll Shelf Award
Children's Book Showcase
Children's Choices
Discovery Award, New York YM–YWHA Poetry Center
Golden Kite Award
International Board on Books for Young People Honor List
Kerlan Award
Coretta Scott King Award
Library of Congress Children's Books of the Year
National Council of Teachers of English Award for
    Excellence in Poetry
National Endowment for the Arts Award
New York Academy of Science Children's Science
    Book Award
New York Times Best Illustrated Children's Books
    of the Year
New York Times Outstanding Books
John Newbery Honor Award
Edgar Allan Poe Award
Pulitzer Prize for Poetry
Rutgers Award
New York Herald Tribune Spring Book Festival

2

Unit 1

Winding Roads

Have you ever walked down a winding road? If you have, you know that you can't see what is ahead. You aren't sure what will happen next. Maybe it will be funny. Maybe it will be exciting.

In each story in "Winding Roads," someone is doing something that is like going down a winding road. No one is sure what lies ahead.

As you read, think about the road each character takes. Think about how each character feels. Think about how you would feel if you were taking that same road.

Read on Your Own

Oscar Otter *by Nathaniel Benchley. Harper.* A beaver's tree destroys Oscar Otter's slide. Oscar builds a new slide far from the safety of home, but the fox is watching him.

Piggle *by Crosby Bonsall. Harper.* Homer looks for someone to play with and finally meets his old friend Bear. They play Piggle, a game of rhyming words.

Aunt Nina and Her Nephews and Nieces *by Franz Brandenberg. Greenwillow.* A treasure hunt to find the birthday cat at Aunt Nina's has a surprise ending.

A Fish in His Pocket *by Denys Cazet. Orchard.* Russell Bear drops his book into the pond and arrives at school with a fish. All day Russell worries about the fish.

The Bear Who Saw the Spring *by Karla Kuskin. Harper.* A small dog meets a bear who takes him on a walk through the seasons in a rhyming story.

The Rooftop Mystery *by Joan M. Lexau. Harper.* Sam loses his sister's big doll. Now he and Albert must follow the clues to find who has taken it.

Mitchell Is Moving *by Marjorie Weinman Sharmat. Macmillan.* Mitchell moves away and misses his friend Margo, but happily she moves next door.

Funny Feet! *by Leatie Weiss. Watts.* A naughty pigeon-toed penguin won't wear her ugly shoes when away from home. She has to make up for lost time when her parents come to see her dance.

Basketball season is about to start and Jeremy is faced with a problem. What is his problem and how does he solve it?

Backyard Basketball Superstar

by Monica Klein

All Jeremy could think about was basketball season. He thought about being captain of his team, the Flyers. Jeremy ran to read the big sign he had put in his front yard.

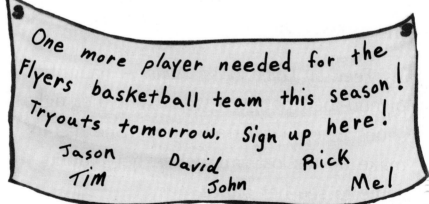

One more player needed for the Flyers basketball team this season!
Tryouts tomorrow. Sign up here!
Jason   David   Rick
Tim   John   Mel

"Oh no!" he said. "It can't be! I don't believe it!"

6

Just then Micky and Adam rode by. "Hi, Jeremy!" said Micky. "How many names are on the list?"

"One too many," said Jeremy. "The last one on this list is *my little sister*!"

"But she can't play basketball," said Adam.

"Just take a look in my backyard," said Jeremy. They all ran to the backyard. They watched Melanie make basket after basket.

"She can play!" said Micky.

"Not on *my* team!" said Jeremy.

"She's taller than anyone on the team," said Adam.

"She's not just tall," said Micky. "She jumps high and runs fast, too."

"She sure can throw a basketball," said Adam, "even if she is a girl."

"She's not just a girl," said Jeremy. "She's my little sister, and she can't play on my team!"

"We'll see you tomorrow," said Adam as he and Micky left.

"Melanie!" Jeremy called. "I bet you're tired, aren't you?"

"Boy, am I ever!" said Melanie.

"Well, since you're so tired, I'll clean your room," said Jeremy.

"You will?" said Melanie.

"Sure," said Jeremy, "and since you're so tired, you won't want to try out for the Flyers tomorrow."

"What?" said Melanie. "I'll be in great shape by tomorrow. I wouldn't miss the tryouts for anything!"

"Not even for my giant ant farm?" asked Jeremy.

"Jeremy, I'm getting the idea that you don't want me to try out for the Flyers," said Melanie.

"I never said that," said Jeremy.

"Don't worry, Jeremy," said Melanie. "You'll be proud of me. I'll play my best at the tryouts."

"I know you will," said Jeremy.

"That's what I'm worried about," Jeremy thought to himself.

Jeremy went inside. He heard Melanie in the yard. *Swish thump! Swish thump!*

"Why does *my* little sister have to be a backyard basketball superstar?" he said to himself. "When Melanie tries out for the team, all the Flyers will laugh at me."

Jeremy sighed and said to himself, "A backyard basketball superstar in my own family, and it's not me."

The next morning everyone met in Jeremy's yard. "Jeremy!" said one of the Flyers. "Your sister wants to try out. You're our captain. Can a girl try out?" Everyone waited for Jeremy's answer.

Jeremy did not say a thing. He thought about being captain and being the best team on the block. He knew what he had to do. He took the ball and threw it into Melanie's hands. "Shoot, Mel," he said. *Swish thump! Swish thump!*

"She sure is good," said Micky.

"Even if she is a girl," said Adam.

"She's not just a girl," Jeremy thought to himself. "She's my little sister! But—she is just the player the Flyers need to be the best team on the block."

After everyone had a chance to try out, Jeremy said, "Let's vote!"

11

Each of the Flyers wrote a name on
a slip of paper and put it in a box.
Then Jeremy opened the box and read
the names.

"We all voted for the same person,"
Jeremy said.

"We did?" said Micky.

"Even you?" asked Adam.

"Yes," said Jeremy. "We all voted
for the one person who can run fast,
jump high, and really throw a
basketball. Welcome to the Flyers, Mel!"

Melanie smiled. She threw the ball
into the basket. *Swish thump!* The
players all knew it would be a very
good basketball season.

1. What was Jeremy's problem, and how did he solve it?

2. Why didn't Jeremy want Melanie to try out to play for the Flyers?

3. Would you like to have Jeremy for a brother? Why?

4. What did Jeremy do that was best for the team?

5. What words are used to show that Melanie shoots baskets well?

6. How was Jeremy's problem like going down a winding road?

Think and Write

Pretend you are Melanie. Write three sentences telling Jeremy why you should try out for the team. Or pretend you are Jeremy. Write three sentences telling why Melanie should <u>not</u> try out for the team.

13

Girls Can, Too!

by Lee Bennett Hopkins

Children's Choices Poet

Tony said: "Boys are better!
  They can . . .

    whack a ball,
    ride a bike with one hand,
    leap off a wall."

I just listened
  and when he was through,
I laughed and said:

 "Oh, yeah! Well, girls can, too!"

Then I leaped off the wall,
  and rode away
With *his* 200 baseball cards
  I won that day.

Exercising can be fun. What are some exercises you can do? Why are these exercises good for you?

"E" Is for Exercise

by Nanette Mason

What exercises do you do? Do you know that when you walk fast, run, swim, or ride your bike, you are really exercising? Do you know that when you jump rope or play tag, you are also exercising?

Do you want to run faster? Would you like to jump higher or throw a ball better? Here are some more exercises that are fun to do and good for you, too.

17

These exercises will help you move better and help make your body strong. Always begin with stretching exercises to help you warm up. Numbers 1-4 are stretching exercises. Numbers 5-7 will help make your body strong.

1. Stand up. Bend down to touch your toes.

2. Sit with your legs out. Reach past your toes.

3. Sit with one leg out. Bend the other leg back. Reach out and try to touch your toes.

4. Stand with your feet flat on the floor. Lock your hands behind your neck. Turn slowly left, then right.

5. Stand with your feet flat on the floor. Then raise and lower your heels.

6. Lie on your back. Bend your knees. Keep your feet flat on the floor. Lock your hands behind your head. Sit up and touch your elbows to your knees.

19

7. Pull yourself up on
an exercise bar, or
hang from it.

When you exercise, the last thing you should do is cool down. Give your body a chance to cool down slowly by doing some more stretching exercises.

If you exercise every day, you will feel good, look good, and be stronger.

1. What are three exercises that you read about?

2. Why are exercises good for you?

3. What would you tell someone who said exercising takes too much time and costs too much money?

4. Find the exercise that could be called "sit-ups." Why would this be a good name?

5. Exercising is fun and good for you, if you start and end the right way. What is the right way to exercise?

Talk with a friend about something you like to do to keep your body strong. Write a paragraph describing what you do. Then have another friend read your paragraph and do what it describes.

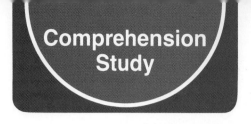

Sequence

The **sequence** of a story is the order in which things happen. Knowing sequence helps you understand better what you read. Sometimes writers use **clue** words to help you follow the order.

Read the paragraph below. Use the underlined clue words to help you understand the sequence.

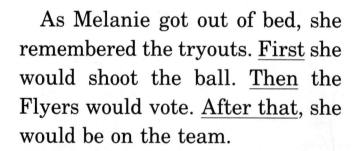

As Melanie got out of bed, she remembered the tryouts. <u>First</u> she would shoot the ball. <u>Then</u> the Flyers would vote. <u>After that</u>, she would be on the team.

Did you notice the clue words *first, then,* and *after that*? These clue words should help you answer some questions about the sequence, or the order of things in Melanie's day.

What was the first thing Melanie would do? She would shoot the ball. How do you know? The clue word is *first*. What would happen next? The Flyers would vote. How do you know? The clue word is *then*. What would happen last? Melanie would be on the team. How do you know? The clue words are *after that*.

Now look for clue words as you read the following paragraph.

Bill's mother left a note for him. The note said, "First, clean your room. Then I want you to go to the store. Please cut the grass after that. You can go swimming later."

Did you find the clue words *first, then, after that,* and *later*? Now answer the following questions and tell how you know. What is Bill to do last? What is Bill to do second? What is the third thing Bill is to do?

Look for clue words when you read. They help you remember the sequence, or the order in which things happen.

Ronald can't seem to do anything right today. What surprise does Ronald get at the end of this day?

Today Was a Terrible Day

by Patricia Reilly Giff

Today was a terrible day. It started when I dropped my pencil. Miss Tyler asked, "Ronald Morgan, why are you crawling under your desk like a snake?" So all the children started to call me Snakey.

When Miss Tyler told us to take out last
night's homework, I noticed that my
mother had forgotten to sign mine. I
quickly signed it for her. Miss Tyler said,
"Ronald Morgan. It is wrong to sign other
people's names. Besides, you spelled your
mother's name wrong." All the children
laughed.

Later, when Billy was reading—he's in
the Satellite group—I got hungry. I was so
hungry that I tiptoed to the coatroom and
ate a sandwich. I had the wrong bag,
however, so I ate Jimmy's sandwich.

"Ronald Morgan, what are you eating?"
Miss Tyler asked.

"A sandwich," I said. "I ate Jimmy's
sandwich by mistake."

All the children looked at me. Jimmy
cried because he didn't want my sandwich.

Then, when Alice was reading—she's in
the Mariners—my group had to do a
workbook page. I didn't remember how to
do it so I asked Rosemary.

"Don't you even know how to do that?"
Rosemary asked. She's in the Rockets
group, just like me.

Later, we went outside to play ball. I
played left field because I don't catch very
well. Only one ball came near me. I ran
for it. I almost had it.

I missed, and my milk money fell out of my pocket. "You just lost the game, Snakey," Billy yelled.

When lunchtime finally came, I had no money for milk. I watched Jimmy eat my sandwich. I was still hungry. All I had was part of Rosemary's carrot and one of Billy's grapes.

After lunch, Miss Tyler called the Rockets to the reading circle. I'm a Rocket. Rosemary read the first sentence. Tom read the next one. They didn't make any mistakes today.

When it was my turn, I said, "Sally was a horse." I was almost sure I hadn't made a mistake.

Miss Tyler said, "Ronald Morgan, you made a mistake."

Rosemary said, "Sally saw a house."

Tom said, "Some Rocket you are."

It was almost time to go home. Miss Tyler said, "I think the plant person has forgotten to water the plants again." Guess who the plant person is?

I got up and watered all the plants. While I was doing the last one, the best one, I looked out the window. Somehow I knocked the pot off the windowsill.

When it was finally time to go home, Miss Tyler gave me a note. "Ronald Morgan," she said. "Take this note home. Try to read it by yourself. If you can't, I'm sure your mother will help you."

On the way home, I read the note.

Guess what? I read that whole note by myself without making any mistakes. I can read. Wait till I tell Michael. He's my best friend.

"Hello, Michael? This is Snakey. Guess what? I just found out I can read. Guess what else? It's Miss Tyler's birthday tomorrow. I think I'll take her a plant. I know she needs one."

1. What surprise did Ronald get at the end of the day?

2. Tell three things that made Ronald's day a terrible one.

3. What did Miss Tyler do to make Ronald feel better?

4. How did you feel when you read Miss Tyler's note to Ronald? Why?

5. When did you begin to think that Ronald's next day might be better?

6. What did Ronald learn about days that seem to be terrible?

Pretend that you are having a terrible day. Make a list of the things that are going wrong. Then write a paragraph about how you could change your day into a happy one.

Predicting Outcomes

When you read you can sometimes **predict,** or tell ahead of time, what is going to happen. You are able to do this by thinking about what has already happened. You think about the people and how they have acted so far.

Think about Ronald in "Today Was a Terrible Day." When he went to water the plants, you knew something terrible was probably going to happen. Ronald's whole day had been one terrible thing after another. Since he was watering plants, you might have thought he would spill the water or knock the plant over.

When you predict, you aren't *sure* what will happen. You are predicting what you think will happen. You need to read on to see if you are right.

Read the paragraph below. Predict what might happen next.

Jane liked to cook out. She had the meat and buns ready. Jane was building the fire. While she worked, her dog played nearby.

What might happen next? Did you predict that her dog might grab the meat? To find out, read on.

As Jane turned to put the meat on to cook, her dog started barking. A strange dog ran off down the street with Jane's meat.

Jane's dog did not grab the meat, but your prediction was still a good one. What happened next did have something to do with a dog. As you read, new clues caused you to change your mind. Now you are ready to predict what might happen because of the strange dog.

As you read stories, try to predict what will happen next. Be ready to change your mind as you read on.

Margaret has a good idea for the school carnival. What is her idea? How does her idea help the school?

The Balancing Girl

by Berniece Rabe

Margaret was very good at balancing. She could balance a book on her head. She could wheel along in her wheelchair as nice as you please. The book would not fall off.

One day Margaret balanced thirty blocks on the floor. "That's simple," Tommy said.

"Then you do it," said Margaret.

Tommy wouldn't try. He just said, "I still say it's simple."

Margaret planned and planned. She wanted to do something very special that Tommy could not call simple. She got out of her wheelchair. She pushed some other chairs together. She made a private corner for her work. It took a long time and great care, but at last she was finished. She had finished a fine castle of blocks.

Tommy said, "That's simple. I build castles like that all the time."

Margaret would have shouted at him, but Ms. Joliet said, "Time for recess."

When they came back into the room after recess, Margaret's castle was knocked down flat!

Tommy was the first person to shout, "I don't know who did it!"

Ms. Joliet had to leave the room just then. It gave Margaret a chance to say, "Tommy, you had better never knock down anything I balance again, or *you'll be sorry*!"

When Ms. Joliet came back, she said, "We are going to hold a school carnival to raise money. We need ideas."

Quickly Tommy raised his hand. "My dad and I could run a fishpond booth. People would pay to fish for prizes." Everyone clapped for Tommy's idea.

"Good," said Ms. Joliet. "Are there any other ideas?"

At the end of the day, Ms. Joliet said, "Each of you put on your thinking cap. See if you can come up with a good idea for the carnival by tomorrow."

Well, it was no trouble at all for Margaret to balance a thinking cap on her head. She thought and thought. The next morning, she said something quietly into Ms. Joliet's ear.

Again Margaret made a private corner. Deep in the corner, she started setting dominoes on end. She placed each domino just a small space away from the last one. She had to be so very, very careful. If anything touched a domino and made it fall, then one by one they would all come falling down.

She soon used all the dominoes, so the next day Ms. Joliet got some more for her. Everybody watched while Margaret made a whole city.

Margaret never saw who dropped a pencil right in the middle of her city. She moaned. "I can't reach into the middle to get it out. One slip and my whole city is gone!"

"I'll get it," said Tommy.

Ms. Joliet stopped him just in time. "I will do it, Tommy." The whole class held their breath. Even Ms. Joliet held her breath as she reached into the middle and got the pencil.

The next day, Margaret finished placing the last domino. Everyone wanted to be the one to push down the first domino. Margaret said, "The name of the person to do that will be pulled out of a hat on the last night of the carnival, *and* you will have to pay to get your name in that hat."

The school carnival was really great. Margaret went to every booth. Then it was time to go to Margaret's corner. A voice said, "Let's move along to the second grade room and see who gets to push down that first domino."

Ms. Joliet waited until everyone was close to Margaret's corner. Then she let the oldest child in the room draw the name from the hat. There wasn't a noise in the room.

Ms. Joliet read,

Tommy pushed to the front. He stepped inside the domino corner. He stood there just looking at Margaret. "Well, push," said Margaret.

Tommy pushed much harder than was needed, but still it went beautifully. Click, click, click. The dominoes took their turns falling. It seemed to take forever for them all to fall. Then a big cheer went up!

Tommy looked right at Margaret and yelled, "There! I knocked down something that you balanced, and I'm not sorry."

"I know you're not," Margaret called back. "Guess what? I made the most money in this whole carnival."

"Hooray! Hooray for the Balancing Girl!" someone shouted. Margaret was sure she heard Tommy join in the big cheer.

1. What was Margaret's idea for the school carnival?

2. How do you know that her idea was a good one?

3. How did Tommy upset Margaret?

4. How did you feel when the pencil was dropped in the domino city? Why?

5. What words on page 40 made you think that people wanted to find out who got to push down the first domino?

Put on your thinking cap. What would be *your* idea for a booth at a school carnival? Write a paragraph about your idea. Then draw a map of your classroom showing how to find your booth.

44

Broom Balancing

by Kathleen Fraser

Millicent can play the flute
and Francine can dance a jig,
but I can balance a broom.

Susanna knows how to bake cookies
and Harold can stand on one foot,
but I can balance a broom.

Jeffry can climb a ladder backwards
and Andrew can count
  to five thousand and two,
but I can balance a broom.

Do you think a circus might discover me?

Margaret used dominoes to build a city. Read to find out other ways dominoes can be used.

What Can You Do with Dominoes?

by Linda Beech

People have been playing with dominoes for a very long time. No one knows just how old dominoes are, but they were used long, long ago in China.

Most domino sets have 28 pieces. The pieces are small and flat. They are almost always black and white. The pieces can stand on edge.

One side of each domino has nothing on it. The other side has two parts. The parts may have small white dots on them, or they may be blank. The dots are called *pips*. This side is used for playing games.

4 pips  **2 pips**

6 pips

The highest number of pips on one piece is 12. That piece has six pips on each part. A piece that has the same number of pips on each part is called a *double domino*. This piece is the double six.

6 pips

double six

The lowest number of pips on a domino is one. This piece has one pip on one part, and the other part is blank.

blank  **1 pip**

One domino in each set has no pips. This is the double blank.

double blank

Many different games can be played with a set of dominoes. Most people play the block game. In this game, the dominoes are placed on a table with the pip side down. Each player takes five pieces. The rest of the dominoes are left in the pile on the table. The players do not show their pieces to the other players.

The player with the highest double domino goes first. That domino is put on the table pip side up. Suppose the first domino is the double three. The next player must play a domino that has three pips on one part. If the player does not have such a piece, then that player must pick from the pile of dominoes until a matching piece is found.

Suppose the second player plays the three-five piece. The third player must use a piece with three or five pips.

2nd player  **1st player**

Look at the picture. What piece did the third player use?

3rd player **2nd player**  **1st player**

Now look at the next picture. It shows how the third player would have played using a piece with three pips on one part.

1st player

2nd player 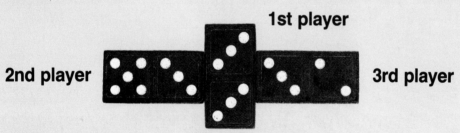 **3rd player**

Notice that double dominoes are always placed in a different way from the other pieces.

As the game goes on, each player tries to match one part of a domino to another. All the players try to be the first to use their pieces.

Some people like to build things with dominoes. Then they like to watch them fall down. If dominoes are set up in rows, they fall down in rows, too,—one by one, faster and faster.

The men in the picture used dominoes to make big shapes and pictures. It took them many weeks to set up the dominoes. Then, with just a small tap, they pushed the first domino. Down went the dominoes, row by row by row!

1. Tell some ways in which dominoes can be used.

2. Tell how the game of dominoes is played.

3. Do you think that this game would be fun to play? Why?

4. What did you read that told you that dominoes is an old game? Find that part of the selection.

5. Why do you think the author wrote this selection?

Think and Write

Think about your favorite game. Think about how it is played, how many people it takes to play it, and what you need to do to win the game. Then write a paragraph explaining the game. Use the paragraph to help you teach the game to a friend.

51

Today is a very special day for Grandpa. What makes this day so special? How does Grandpa feel about this special day?

My Grandpa Retired Today

by Elaine Knox-Wagner

My Grandpa retired today. I was the only kid at the party. "Come have some juice, Margey," Grandpa said. So I did. We never have juice at the barbershop. It was very good.

52

Then I oiled the barber chairs and
moved them up and down. I swept up
black hair and brown hair and a little
red hair.

Grandpa was talking and laughing
with all the men. I pulled on his arm.
"Should I wash the combs?" I asked.

"Not yet. Why don't you throw out
all the old newspapers," he said. I
saluted. He saluted. It's an old game
we play.

I threw the old newspapers into the
trash can. I wiped off all the cans and
bottles and lined them up.

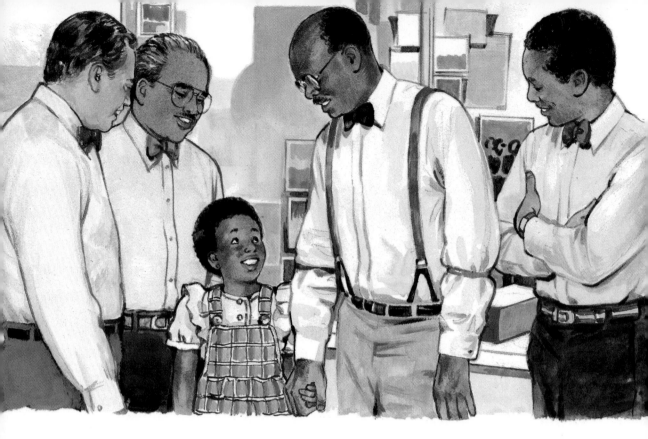

Grandpa stood in a circle of tall
men. Some I didn't even know. I stood
on a chair and waved at him over
their heads. He waved back. I slipped
through the circle and took Grandpa's
hand. He smiled at me. His friends
smiled at me.

Grandpa's friend, Joe, slapped him on
the back. "Well, Al," he said, "time
for the big surprise."

"Tata-ta-ta!" someone yelled. We all
turned to look.

Someone had tied a giant red bow
around the barber chair with Grandpa's
name on the back. "Because no one can
take your place, Al, we want you to
take this chair with you," said Joe.
Everyone clapped. Grandpa just stared.

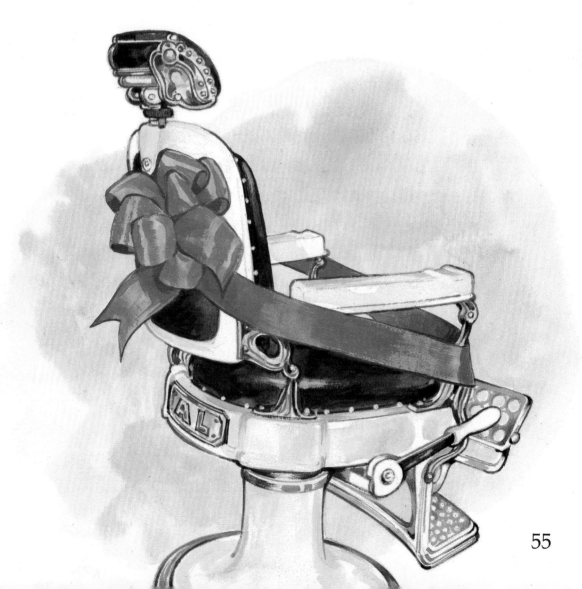

Soon the men were gone, the "Closed" sign was in the window, and Grandpa's barber chair was driving away in the back of a truck.

"Well, let's give the place a last clean-up, then," he said. We filled some of the bottles. We put the combs in to be washed. We did everything we could think to do. At last, it was time to leave.

"Do you want to lock up?" Grandpa asked.

"You do it today," I said.

We walked home slowly. I kicked a stone and sighed. Grandpa kicked a stone and sighed. We waited for a green light.

"This might be fine weather for the beach," Grandpa said.

"I like barbershops," I said. The light changed.

"Then again, we always did mean to get downtown to see those dinosaur bones," he said.

"You can see them in books," I said.

Grandpa took my hand. "I sure will miss the shop," he said.

"Me, too," I said.

When I went to say good night, Grandpa was in his room, sitting in the barber chair that said "Al" on the back. His eyes were closed, and he looked lonesome. I climbed onto his lap. "There is more to life than working in a barbershop," I said.

Grandpa laughed and laughed and laughed. So I laughed and laughed and laughed. "I don't know where you pick up some of the things you say," he told me.

"From you, mostly," I said.

"Off to bed with you now," he said. "We've got things to do tomorrow."

1. What made the day special for Margey's grandpa?

2. Would you miss the barbershop if you were Grandpa? If you were Margey? Explain your answer.

3. How did Margey help Grandpa feel better? What else could she have done to help?

4. When did you learn why the chair was given to Grandpa?

5. Margey and her grandpa will find new ways to enjoy life. What could they do?

Think and Write

Pretend you are going to talk to a person who is retired. What are some questions you might ask that person? Write your questions. Then have a friend pretend to be the retired person and answer your questions.

Thinking About "Winding Roads"

In the stories in "Winding Roads," you read about characters on many different roads. These characters did not know what they would find as they started, but they went on anyway.

Mel and Jeremy each tried something new, and it turned out just fine. Ronald was having a terrible day, but on his way home from school he discovered he could read. Margaret would not let anything stop her from trying something new. Margey and her grandfather looked forward to a different life after Grandpa retired.

As you read other stories, think about how the characters sometimes find themselves on a winding road. Think about how the characters in the stories face new things in their lives.

1. How are Melanie and Margaret the same? How are they different?

2. Was Ronald's day like Margey's day? Why?

3. Do you think Tommy from "The Balancing Girl" would be good friends with Jeremy from "Backyard Basketball Superstar"? Why?

4. Which character in this unit followed the most interesting winding road? Why do you think so?

Unit 2

Mountaintops

Do you think you would like to climb a mountain? How do you think you would feel when you got to the mountaintop?

Some people say that they have reached a mountaintop when they feel very good about something they have done. In each story in "Mountaintops," someone has reached a goal or solved a problem. Each character feels good about something.

As you read, think about the goals the characters reach or the problems they solve. Think about how they feel when they reach their mountaintops.

Read on Your Own

Who's a Pest? *by Crosby Newell Bonsall. Harper.* Homer proves that he is not a pest when he saves the day and makes a friend.

Frosted Glass *by Denys Cazet. Bradbury.* Gregory Dog can't draw a circle. When the teacher tells the class to draw flowers, Gregory makes his picture into a rocket ship.

The Goose Who Wrote a Book *by Judy Delton. Carolrhoda Bks.* Goose follows the advice of her friends and changes her book, but the publishing company likes it best the way Goose wrote it.

Little Black, a Pony *by Walter Farley. Beginner Books.* Little Black is sad when his boy rides Big Red, but then the boy and Big Red fall through the ice.

Nobody Listens to Andrew *by Elizabeth Guilfoile. Modern Curriculum.* Andrew has something important to say, but no one will listen. Then he shouts that there is a bear on his bed.

Okay, Good Dog *by Ursula Landshoff. Harper.* It is hard to train a dog, but it will make you and your dog happy.

Hill of Fire *by Thomas P. Lewis. Harper.* This true story is about Pablo and his family. They live a simple life in Mexico until the earth opens up and a volcano erupts on their farm.

Henry and Mudge in the Green Time *by Cynthia Rylant. Bradbury.* Henry and his dog Mudge have a wonderful summer. They even climb a hill to fight dragons and then sleep under a magic tree.

Jasper wants something very much.
Does Jasper get what he wants?
If so, how does he do it?

Jasper and the Hero Business

by Betty Horvath

Jasper lived in the house on the corner. It was a busy corner. All day long people passed by, hurrying to work and then hurrying home again.

Jasper didn't hurry. He didn't have any place to go. Sometimes he didn't have anything to do. He just sat and watched the people pass by. Sometimes people stopped and talked to Jasper. They asked him questions.

66

The little boy took the money. He didn't say anything. He just watched Jasper and Rover go into the house.

"Maybe I'm going about this hero business all wrong," thought Jasper.

"Do you know any heroes?" he asked his mother.

"Look out the window," said his mother. "There is a hero coming up the walk this very minute."

Jasper ran to the window. "That's just Father," he said. "I never knew he was a hero."

"There are all kinds of heroes," said his mother. "Your father worked hard today to earn money to pay the rent and the food bill. Maybe he would have liked to do something else."

"Then I will put his picture on my hero board," said Jasper. Jasper put a picture of his father on his hero board. Then he pinned his mother's picture next to it. There was still the place where Jasper's picture belonged. He was getting older every minute. Another day was almost gone. Jasper wasn't a hero yet.

While they were eating supper, the doorbell rang. Jasper's father answered the door and came back carrying a bunch of flowers. "These are for you," he said.

"Jasper has a girlfriend!" said Paul.

"No," said his father, "it was a little boy. He said Jasper gave him money."

"Oh, *him*!" said Jasper. "I *found* some money, but it was his. So I just gave it to him."

Nobody said anything for a minute. Then Paul said, "I bet that little boy thinks Jasper is a hero."

"Who, me? A hero?"

"Sure," said Paul. "If somebody thinks you're a hero, you are one. It is time to pin your picture on the hero board."

Paul helped him pin the picture on the board. Under it they wrote "Jasper the Hero." The board was finished now. There was no more space. "Now that you are a hero," said Paul, "what are you going to be next?"

"You don't ever stop being a hero," said Jasper, "but maybe I'll be something else, too. I think I'll be a hero and work on being a doctor. What are you going to be?"

"Me?" asked Paul. "I'm going to be busy trying not to get sick!"

1. What did Jasper want?

2. Jasper thought he had to do something dangerous to be a hero. What did he find out?

3. Name three people who were heroes in the story and tell why.

4. What made Jasper finally decide he was a hero?

5. How do you feel about Jasper's brother? Why?

6. When in the story did Jasper learn that there are different kinds of heroes?

Make a hero board. Cut out pictures from magazines or newspapers of people that you think of as your heroes. Glue the pictures to a piece of paper. Write under each picture why that person is your hero.

The Question

by Karla Kuskin

People always say to me
"What do you think you'd like to be
When you grow up?"
And I say, "Why,
I think I'd like to be the sky
Or be a plane or train or mouse
Or maybe a haunted house
Or something furry, rough and wild . . .
Or maybe I will stay a child."

Nate is a detective who has a case to solve. What clues does Nate use as he tries to solve this case?

Nate the Great and the Missing Key

by Marjorie Weinman Sharmat

I, Nate the Great, am a detective. I am not afraid of anything, except for one thing. Today I am going to a birthday party for the one thing I am afraid of—Annie's dog, Fang.

This morning my dog, Sludge, and I were getting ready for the party. The doorbell rang. I opened the door. Annie and Fang were there. "I need help," Annie said. "I can't find the key to my house. I can't get in to have the birthday party for Fang."

I, Nate the Great, was sorry about the
key and glad about the party. I said, "Tell
me about your key."

"Well," Annie said, "the last time I saw
it was when I went out to get Fang a
birthday surprise to eat."

"To eat?" I said.

"Yes," Annie said. "That's the one
present I had forgotten to buy. I got
Fang lots of presents. I got him a new
collar with a license number, a silver
name tag, and a little silver bone to
hang from the collar. See how pretty
Fang looks."

I, Nate the Great, did not want to
look at Fang. "Tell me more," I said.

"Well, Rosamond and her four cats were at my house," Annie said. "When I went to the store, I left Rosamond and the cats in my house. I left Fang in the yard. I left the key to my house on a table. That is the last time I saw the key. When I got back, Fang was still in the yard, but the house was locked. Rosamond and her cats were gone. Rosamond left this note."

Your key can be found
At a place that is round
A place that is safe
And where things are shiny.
A place that is big
Because it's not tiny.
And this is a poem.
And I went home.

"That is a strange poem," I said.
"Sometimes Rosamond is strange," Annie said.

I, Nate the Great, knew that. "You
must ask Rosamond where she put
your key."

"I went to her house," Annie said.
"No one was home."

I, Nate the Great, said, "I will take
your case."

I wrote a note to my mother.

Dear Mother,

I am on a case.
I am looking for a
round, safe, shiny, big
place. When I find it,
I will be back.

Love,
Nate the Great

Annie, Fang, Sludge, and I went to Annie's house. "What does your key look like?" I asked.

"It is silver and shiny," Annie said. Sludge and I looked around. There were many places to leave a key. They were not round, safe, shiny, and big.

"I will have to look in other places," I said.

"Fang and I will wait for you here," Annie said. I, Nate the Great, was glad to hear that.

Sludge and I started walking. All at once I saw a big, safe place. It was a bank. I knew there were many round, shiny things in a bank. Sludge and I walked inside.

"Do you want to put some money in the bank?" the guard asked.

I said, "Did anyone strange with four cats leave a key here?" The guard pointed to the door. Sludge and I left.

Now I, Nate the Great, knew where I should not look for the key. A bank was not a strange enough place for a strange person like Rosamond to leave a key.

I sat down to rest beside a trash can. I had an idea. A trash can would be a strange enough place for Rosamond to hide a key! Now I, Nate the Great, knew that I had to look in Annie's trash can.

Sludge and I walked to the trash can behind Annie's house. I tried to pull up the cover. Sludge tried to push up the cover with his nose. I pulled harder. Sludge pushed harder. We looked inside the can. There was nothing there.

I, Nate the Great, had not solved the case. Sludge and I went home.

I was very hungry. I made pancakes. I sat down to eat them, but I did not have a fork. I opened a drawer. It was full of spoons and knives and forks all together in a shiny silver pile. I had to look in the drawer a long time before I found a fork. It is hard to find something silver and shiny when it is mixed in with other things that are silver and shiny.

I, Nate the Great, thought about that. Maybe Annie's key was someplace where nobody would see it because it was with other shiny silver things. Now I, Nate the Great, knew the place!

Sludge and I went back to Annie's
house. "I know where your key is," I said.

"Where?" Annie asked.

"Look at Fang's collar," I said.

Annie looked. "I see Fang's license
hanging on his collar," she said. "I see
his silver name tag. I see his silver bone
and—my key!"

"Yes. I, Nate the Great, say that
Rosamond hung your key on Fang's
collar. We did not notice it because
there were other silver things there."

"But why did Rosamond hang it there?"
Annie asked.

I said, "That's easy. Remember
Rosamond's poem? Well, Fang's collar is
round. The things hanging on it are shiny.
Fang is big. There is no place more safe
to leave a key than a few inches from
Fang's teeth. No one would try to take off
that key, not even me." I started to leave.

"Wait!" Annie said. She took the key
from Fang's collar. "Now I can have my
party, and you can come!"

I, Nate the Great, was glad for Annie
and sorry for me. We all went inside.
Annie gave me the best seat because I
had solved the case. It was next to Fang.
I, Nate the Great, hoped it would be a
very short party.

1. What are some clues that Nate used to find the missing key?

2. Why did Rosamond write a poem?

3. How did you feel about where Nate sat at Fang's party?

4. How was the problem or mystery finally solved?

5. What did you read on page 82 that made Nate think that the bank was a good place to look for the key?

Rosamond hid the key in a good hiding place. Pretend that you are going to hide a key in your classroom. Write clues so that a friend can solve the mystery. You may wish to write your clues as a poem.

Multiple-meaning Words

If someone asks you what the word *case* means, you might have a hard time answering. It could mean "a problem needing a detective." It could also mean "a box to keep things in, such as a case of dog food." You need to know how the word is used to know what it means.

When Nate the Great says, "I will take your case," *case* means "a problem needing a detective." How a word is used helps you to know its meaning. The other words in the sentence or story are clues.

Now read the following sentences.

1. Nate wrote a <u>note</u> to his mother.

2. Nate couldn't sing a <u>note</u>.

3. Please <u>note</u> what I tell you.

What does *note* mean in the first sentence? It means "something you write to someone." The other words in the sentence help you know the meaning.

What does *note* mean in the second sentence? The word *sing* helps you know that in this sentence the word *note* has something to do with music.

In the third sentence, what does *note* mean? The other words help you know that *note* means "listen to carefully."

When you know more than one meaning for a word, you must choose the meaning that makes sense. The word *safe* can mean "not able to be hurt," or "a place where money can be locked up." Which meaning does the word *safe* have in the following sentence? *The money was in the safe.*

When a word has more than one meaning, choose the meaning that makes sense in the sentence or story.

The big goat can't sneeze. Why is this a problem? How is the goat's problem solved?

The Goat Who Couldn't Sneeze

*A Mexican folktale
retold by Philip D. Jordan*

The animals all came together to help the goat who couldn't sneeze.

He was a big, grown-up goat with a fine set of curled horns. His coat was as white as the snow that covers the mountains.

All the other goats could sneeze *kerchoo*, but this goat just couldn't. His nose would begin to tickle. He could feel a sneeze coming on. Then, when he threw back his head, and was all ready to sneeze, nothing happened.

"I don't see why you can't sneeze,"
said the big bear crossly. "You do it like
this." He sneezed a sneeze that shook
the mountains. It rang through the
valleys.

The deer said, "I can't understand why
you can't sneeze. It's very simple." The
deer sneezed a polite, dainty sneeze.

"I've sneezed ever since I was a
kitten," said the wildcat. She licked her
paw. "There's really nothing to it."

"I know." The goat hung his big head. "I try. I try very hard." He drew back his lips. He sucked in air until his eyes watered. He tickled his nose with a hoof. "I think—I think I'm going to now." He puffed and gasped, but nothing came out. "I can't," he cried. "I just can't. I never could!"

The other goats wouldn't have a leader who couldn't sneeze. One by one, all the other goats left the big goat.

They didn't as much as say *adiós*.

The bear said he had business in his cave. He thumped away, setting small stones rolling under his big feet.

The wildcat and the dainty deer guessed it was about time for lunch. They started down a pass to the grass meadows.

The big goat was left all alone.

The sun went down, and the moon
came up. When morning touched the
mountain peak, the big goat packed his
bag. He went quietly past the bear's
cave. The sun shone brightly, and the
goat felt happier.

"I'm going to town to learn to sneeze.
To sneeze, to sneeze, to sneeze," he
sang.

After a while, he came to a market
village.

"*Buenos días*—good morning," he
said to a woman selling baskets. "I've
come to learn how to sneeze."

"Well, I can't teach you. I'm too busy. Besides, I only sneeze when I have a cold. Then I cover my nose."

"Buenos días," the goat said to the miller grinding corn for *tortillas.* "Can you tell me how to sneeze, please?" The miller just went on grinding, for this was market day.

"Buenos días," said the goat to the schoolmaster. "I do so much want to learn how to sneeze. Will you teach me?"

"I have more work than I know how to do now," answered the schoolmaster. He closed the school door.

The goat who couldn't sneeze picked up his bag. He started down the winding road.

He walked and he walked and he walked. By and by he sat down to rest. He propped his back against a tree and rubbed his hoofs, because they were sore from walking. *Caballeros* on horses rode by, but they didn't speak to the goat.

"What are you doing here?" buzzed a strange voice.

At first the goat who couldn't sneeze thought he was dreaming. He thought he was hearing a voice in his head. But there was a voice. It was coming from a honey bee in a golden brown and black jacket.

"What are you doing here? You belong up on the mountain peak." The bee settled down, so the goat could see him better.

"I came down to learn how to sneeze," said the goat, "but no one will show me how."

"Learn how to sneeze?" The bee was surprised.

"I'm the only goat who can't sneeze," the big goat said.

The bee asked, "Why can't you sneeze? Do you try?"

"Of course. Of course, I try."

"Well, I can teach you to sneeze," said the bee.

"You can?"

The bee answered, "Of course I can."

"Do it then. Show me how," cried the goat.

The bee in the golden brown and black jacket flew into the air. He made a loop and settled down right on the goat's nose.

"Can you see me?" asked the bee. He began to dance little tickle steps.

The goat looked down his nose. All he saw was a blur of black and golden brown.

He started to say "No." Then his nose began to tickle, to t-i-c-k-l-e, to *tickle*.

He just couldn't say anything!

His lips drew back. Tears ran down
his beard. His mouth opened. Out came
a big *ker-choo*. And another. And another.

They were the loudest sneezes ever
heard in those parts.

"I knew it. I knew it," buzzed the bee.
"I knew I could teach you to sneeze!
Now try it again."

The big goat did. This time he sneezed so loud that the people in the village heard the noise and thought it was thunder.

"I can sneeze any time I want to now," said the happy goat. "I've learned!"

"Of course you can," said the bee, and flew away.

From that day to this, a mountain goat always sneezes when he sees a bee in a golden brown and black jacket.

Discuss the Selection

1. Why is not knowing how to sneeze a problem for the goat?

2. How is the goat's problem solved?

3. What did you think about the characters who would not help the goat?

4. When did you first think that the goat was going to learn to sneeze?

5. The goat probably didn't think a bee would teach him to sneeze. What do you think the goat learned about how problems are solved?

Think and Write

Pretend you are the storyteller. Think about another character the goat may have asked for help. Use your imagination and write what the goat and your character might say to each other. Remember to use *Buenos días*.

Sally Ride wanted to circle the earth, and she did. Read to find out what she has to say about that trip.

Sally Ride, Astronaut – An American First

from a book by June Behrens

5 . . . 4 . . . 3 . . . 2 . . . 1 . . . 0 . . . Lift-off! Spacecraft *Challenger* lifted off from Cape Canaveral, Florida. Up into the air it climbed. In a few minutes, it was out of sight.

This was *Challenger*'s second trip into space. One of the five astronauts on this flight was Sally Ride. Sally was the first American woman to go into space. She was also the youngest American astronaut to circle the earth.

While in space, each astronaut had important work to do. Sally Ride's job was to test a robot arm. She was to find out how well the arm worked. This was the first time the robot arm was to be used in space. On later trips, the arm would be used to pick up satellites in trouble.

Challenger's second flight lasted six days. Then the spacecraft returned to Earth. It landed in California.

Sally Ride had grown up in California
not far from where *Challenger* landed.
While Sally was growing up, she worked
hard to be good at whatever she did.
Sally had always been interested in
the stars and planets. She studied
about them in school.

One day Sally read in the newspaper that men and women were wanted for the space program. They would learn to be astronauts. Many, many people wanted to be part of the space program. However, only thirty-five were picked for the 1978 astronaut class. Sally Ride was one of the six women picked.

Sally moved to Texas to begin her training as an astronaut. She learned to fly airplanes. She learned about flying a spacecraft. She learned to work the robot arm. Sally learned all the things an astronaut needs to know.

U.S. AIR FORCE T-38A NO-80
A.F. SERIAL NO. 69-7084
SERVICE THIS AIRCRAFT WITH GRADE
JP-4 FUEL IF NOT AVAILABLE TO NO
42B1-1-14 WILL BE CONSULTED FOR

1. PUSH
2. PULL

The very best astronauts were needed for the second *Challenger* flight. These people would have to work as a team. Sally Ride was picked as part of the second *Challenger* team. This team worked very hard to get ready for the flight.

On June 18, 1983, the whole world watched as *Challenger* lifted off. Sally Ride made news.

"The thing that I'll remember most about the flight is that it was fun. In fact, I'm sure it was the most fun that I'll ever have in my life," said Sally Ride.

1. How did Sally Ride feel about her trip into space?

2. Why is Sally Ride an American "first"?

3. Why do you think Sally was picked as part of the *Challenger* team?

4. How did you feel when Sally was picked to go into the astronaut class? Why?

5. What did you read on page 105 that made you think that other people wanted the same job as Sally?

Pretend that you are on a trip through space. Use a piece of paper and pretend that you are sending a postcard to a friend. Draw a picture of your favorite sight from space on one side. Write a note on the other side describing your trip.

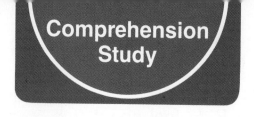

Main Idea and Details

The **main idea** is the most important idea of a paragraph. It tells what the paragraph is about. Sometimes the main idea is in the first sentence of a paragraph. Sometimes it is in the last sentence. The main idea may also be in any other sentence in a paragraph. The other sentences in a paragraph give **details** about the main idea.

Read the following paragraph. Find the main idea sentence.

Sally Ride learned how to fly airplanes. She learned about flying a spacecraft. She learned to work the robot arm. She learned what an astronaut needs to know.

The main idea of the paragraph is that Sally Ride learned what an astronaut needs to know. The main idea is in the last sentence of the paragraph. The other sentences give details about learning to be an astronaut.

Now find the main idea in the paragraph below.

Most people enjoy a Fourth of July parade. There are many kinds of parades. Some parades are held to celebrate New Year's Day. Some tell that the circus is in town. Some parades welcome heroes home.

Did you see that the main idea is in the second sentence? The main idea is that there are many kinds of parades. The other sentences give details about kinds of parades.

Remember, looking for the main idea and details will help you understand better what you read.

Each day you see clouds in the sky. Read to find out what clouds are and how they are formed.

Cloudy Weather

by Anne Maley

If you were up in space, you could see Earth floating like a big ball. If you came closer, you could see the clouds that cover Earth. If you came closer still, you could see that Earth is made of land and water.

Have you ever wondered what makes the clouds above Earth? The answer is in the air around you.

Water in the Air

The air is a wonderful collector. It collects bits of dust and smoke. Most of all, it collects water. As it moves over Earth, the air takes water from oceans and lakes. It also takes water from plants and soil. Did you know that the air even collects water from *you*? Here is one way it happens.

Suppose you are wet from swimming. You sit down to dry. As the sun dries you, it turns the water on your body into a gas called water vapor. The water vapor floats into the air, like tiny bubbles you can't see. As the bubbles float higher and higher, they grow colder and colder. When they become cold enough, the bits of vapor turn back into drops of water. Each drop forms around a tiny bit of dust. Many drops of water cling together to form a cloud.

Clouds in the Sky

Clouds are everywhere in the sky. Some are very high in the sky. Some float lower in the sky. Others are even closer to the ground. The highest clouds are the coldest ones. These clouds are made of little bits of ice.

One good place to look for a cloud is on top of a mountain. Can you guess why you might find a cloud there? The answer is that air always grows colder as it moves up the side of a mountain. When the air reaches the top of the mountain, the water vapor has become little drops of water that form a cloud.

As the sun shines on this cloud, the cloud looks warm and bright. If you were to climb through a cloud, though, it would feel cold, dark, and very wet.

Clouds on the Ground

Did you know that you could walk through a cloud without climbing a mountain? When you walk in fog, you are in a cloud that is on the ground.

When air is filled with water, it is called heavy air. Fog may form when heavy air near the ground cools. The water vapor in the air turns into big drops of water or ice. When the sun warms the air, the fog goes away.

Clouds and the Weather

Each kind of weather has its own kind of clouds. Some people watch the clouds to guess what kind of weather is coming. How good are you at watching clouds? Do you know that white, puffy clouds high in the sky often mean good weather? Dark, puffy, flat-bottomed clouds low in the sky often mean rain.

When it rains, the clouds give back much of the water the air has collected. The water soaks into the ground. It fills oceans and lakes. It makes puddles. Soon the puddles go away again. Where do they go?

You know the answer to that question!

1. What are clouds, and how are they made?

2. Water is in the air. Name three things that can make this happen.

3. Where can clouds be found?

4. What did you learn that you didn't know before?

5. How many parts does this selection have? What tells you this?

Keep a weather chart for one week. See for yourself if white puffy clouds mean good weather and dark clouds mean rain. List the days of the week on the side of your paper. Next to each day, write the kind of cloud that you see and what the weather is for that day.

How to Tell the Top of a Hill

by John Ciardi

National Council of Teachers of English
Award Poet

The top of a hill
Is not until
The bottom is below.
And you have to stop
When you reach the top
For there's no more UP to go.

To make it plain
Let me explain:
The one *most* reason why
You have to stop
When you reach the top—is:
The next step up is sky.

In "Cloudy Weather," you read about how clouds are formed. As Nina and her mother climb a mountain, they walk through a cloud. What does Nina discover about the cloud?

The Cloud

Story and pictures by Deborah Kogan Ray

The sky was orange behind the mountain when Nina woke up. She listened to the forest sounds around her. "What will we see on our walk, Mama?" asked Nina.

Her mother answered, "I can't really say, Nina. Every walk is different. We're going to walk all the way up this mountain. We're going to walk so high into the sky that we might even walk right into a cloud."

Nina thought about what it would be like to walk in a cloud. Maybe the cloud would be as soft as a pillow.

Nina looked at the steep hill. It seemed so high. She wondered how they would ever be able to climb such a steep hill.

They crossed a stream and started to climb up the path. They climbed higher and higher. The path went around and around and up. Nina's legs hurt. She felt hot and sticky. She thought she might cry.

Mama stopped. She wiped Nina's face. "You're a real climber, Nina. We just went all around the mountain. It's just a little farther to the top."

They climbed higher and higher still. They climbed past the tall trees. Finally, they reached the top of the mountain.

"Wow, did we ever walk far up," Nina said. "There must be a lot of clouds to walk in, way up here." She looked up at the sky, but she didn't see any clouds. There was no wind. Nothing moved.

Nina looked way down. A valley
stretched far below. When she looked
toward one end of the valley, she saw
trees that looked as small as baby
plants. Past the trees she saw a lake
that looked like a tiny puddle of water.

When Nina looked toward the other
end of the valley, she saw something
strange. It looked like a giant white
pillow. "Look, Mama. What's that?"

"That's a cloud," Mama answered.

Nina wondered about the way it looked. She had seen lots of clouds before. "It doesn't look like a cloud. It's not in the right place. It should be up in the sky. It shouldn't be under us," she said.

"It is in the sky, Nina. We've just climbed so high we're over the clouds."

"Is that cloud coming our way? Will I be able to walk in it?" Nina asked.

"I think so," Mama said. "That cloud is blowing this way pretty fast. We are going to walk down the path into the valley to get to that lake."

Nina looked. The cloud was almost right under them. "I can't wait," she said. The cloud looked cottony soft.

Mama led her back to the path. They started to walk down the mountain. The path was very rocky. Nina shivered. "When will we be in the cloud, Mama?"

"We are in the cloud now," Mama said. "It's blowing a lot of cold air on us."

"We can't be in that cottony white cloud," Nina said. "This is cold and ugly." Nina looked back. All she could see was gray mist. She shivered again and put her hands into her pockets.

"I don't like this. I'm cold, Mama." Nina shook her head. "This isn't pretty. This isn't what I see when I look at the sky. Inside the cloud should look nice. It shouldn't feel this way."

Nina wished the walk would end.

Mama said softly, "Come on, Nina. Let's stay warm together." Mama put her arm around Nina.

They walked down the path on the side of the mountain. Down and down they went, into the valley. "Now the trees are keeping the cloud from blowing the cold air on us," said Mama. The air felt warmer. The sky grew lighter.

"I didn't think the cloud would be like it was when we were walking down the mountain," Nina said. "I was scared, Mama."

Mama kissed Nina. "I know you were, Nina."

"Now the cloud is so pretty," Nina said. She held out her hands in the floating mist. She walked away from Mama. "Look, Mama," she laughed. "I'm walking in a cloud."

1. What did Nina think the cloud would be like? Why?

2. What did Nina discover about the cloud?

3. Name two things that made Nina unhappy.

4. How did you feel about Nina when she was afraid?

5. When in the story did you first begin to think that Nina would not like the cloud?

Think and Write

Nina thought the cloud looked as soft as a pillow and the lake looked like a puddle of water. Think about things you have seen on a walk. Write about them, comparing them to something else as Nina did.

Thinking About "Mountaintops"

You have just read about characters who reached a goal or solved a problem. Each one felt very good about something he or she had done. When people have done something they feel very good about, we sometimes say they have reached a mountaintop.

Jasper found that he could be a hero right at home. Nate used clues to solve the problem of the missing key. The goat reached his goal with some help and was able to return to the other goats. Sally Ride became a hero in space. Nina climbed a real mountain.

As you read other stories, think about how the characters in the stories are trying to reach a goal or solve a problem. Think about how you would feel if you were in the same place.

1. What might Jasper think of Sally Ride? Why?

2. What do you think Nate the Great would have done if he had found the money Jasper found?

3. How are the goat who couldn't sneeze and Nina the same? How are they different?

4. Which character in this unit had the hardest mountaintop to reach? Why do you think so?

Unit 3

Bridges

You know that bridges help us get from one place to another. Did you know that bridges are also ways for us to reach out to other people?

When we meet someone who is different from us, we say that we need a bridge of understanding. By this we mean that we need a way to help us get to know others better.

As you read the stories in this unit, think about the bridges the characters have built to others. Think about why they needed to build a bridge of understanding.

Read on
Your Own

My Hands, My World *by Catherine Brighton. Macmillan.* A blind girl sees the world through her other senses and shares everything with her imaginary friend.

The Real Hole *by Beverly Cleary. Morrow.* Four-year-old Jimmy does not want to pretend that the hole he dug is useful. Daddy solves the problem.

The Boy Who Didn't Believe in Spring *by Lucille Clifton. Dutton.* A boy who lives in the city doesn't believe in spring. He decides to go out and look for it.

The Oldest Kid *by Elaine Knox-Wagner. Whitman.* The oldest kid has to share with and take care of the others, but Grandpa makes things easier by letting his Pal do very important jobs that only the oldest kid could do.

The Homework Caper *by Joan M. Lexau.*
Harper. Ken solves the mystery of his
friend Bill's missing homework and
solves a problem for his little sister at
the same time.

The Great Big Dummy *by Janet Schulman.*
Greenwillow. Anna has no one to play
with, so she makes herself a playmate.

Crow Boy *by Taro Yashima. Viking.* In a village
school in Japan, a small boy is made
fun of by his classmates because he is
quiet and different. An understanding
teacher finds the boy's talent and helps
him share it with others.

The Bear's Water Picnic *by John Yeoman.*
Atheneum. Bear's picnic is disrupted by
the noisy frogs, but later the frogs come
to the rescue.

Do you think it is better to a big sister or a little sister? What do Penny and Lizzie decide?

Little Boss

by Barbara Bottner

"I can't wait until next week," yel Lizzie.

"I can," said Penny. "Everyone is making such a big fuss over you. Mother is making a big fuss. Father is making a big fuss. You are making the biggest fuss of all, just because next week is your birthday."

"Being six is important," said Lizzie.

"Well," Penny said. "Someone else is having a birthday next week, too. Me! Penny! I'll be eight!"

"Eight is too old to make a fuss over," Lizzie said.

"That's the trouble," said Penny. "Nobody is even making a little fuss, just because I'm the big sister."

"Okay, I'll make a little fuss. *Hooray!*" said Lizzie.

"*Hooray* yourself." Penny flopped down on the bed. "When I was six, all we had at my party were dumb balloons. You are getting balloons and special prizes at your party. I'll have to help, just like always. It is no fun being the big sister!"

"Don't you want to know what I want for my birthday?" Lizzie yelled. "I want a two-wheeler. I want a skateboard like Jenny's. I want a horse."

"Could you please not yell," said Penny. "Doesn't anyone want to know what I want for my birthday?"

"Not really."

"Well, I am going to tell you anyway," said Penny. "I want a big sister. I'm tired of being the grown-up one."

"But then you won't be the boss anymore," Lizzie said.

"Being the boss isn't everything," said Penny. "If I fall, I am not supposed to cry. If you fall, you can cry. Everyone feels sorry for you.

"If I want to sit on Daddy's lap, he tells me I am getting too big. If you want to sit on Daddy's lap, you climb up and go to sleep. It's not fair."

"What's the matter?" asked Lizzie.

"Nothing is the matter."

"Don't you want to do the dinosaur puzzle?" Lizzie asked.

"Not really," Penny said.

"What do you want to do then?"

"I want to be the little sister!"

"Okay," said Lizzie. "I'll be the big sister."

"Hah!"

"I will. I know how," said Lizzie.

"Okay, smarty, we will see how you like it. Let's do the dinosaur puzzle."

Lizzie yelled, "Why are you dropping the pieces all over?"

"That is what little sisters do with puzzles," Penny told her. "You have to pick them up. You are the big sister."

While Lizzie was looking for the pieces, Penny said, "I will get some juice."

"Help!" Penny yelled. "I spilled it." Lizzie ran to get a rag.

"My shirt is all wet," Penny yelled. "I need a clean one." Lizzie brought a shirt.

"Clean me up first," Penny told her. "I am all sticky." Lizzie cleaned Penny up. "Help me put my shirt on," Penny said.

"Can't you do anything?" Lizzie asked.

"Well," Penny said. "How do you like being the big sister so far?"

"It's not so bad," answered Lizzie.

"Okay, then. Let's jump rope," Penny said. *Whoosh-thump. Whoosh-thump.*

"What's the matter? Why are you jumping like that?" asked Lizzie. "You are going to fall."

"That is how little sisters jump," Penny said. "If I fall, you will have to pick me up. You are the big sister."

Kerthunk. "Help!" yelled Penny. "My knee is really bleeding! It hurts!"

"Yick!" Lizzie said. She ran away.

"I should have known!" yelled Penny. "You don't know how to be the big sister. You are just a baby."

Penny looked down at her knee. She cried and cried and cried. "At least when you are the little sister, you can cry as much as you want," Penny thought. Then she felt better.

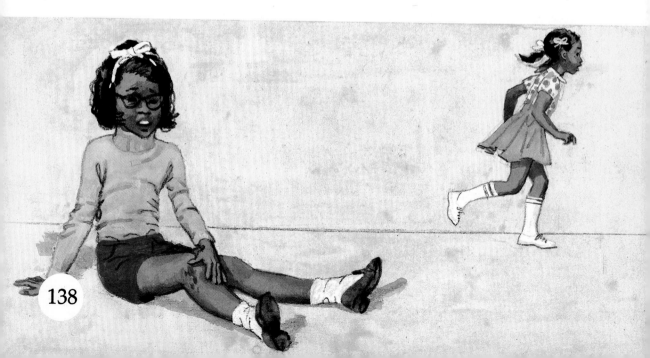

138

Lizzie came back pulling a wagon. "Get in," she said. She pulled Penny to her room.

"Lie down," Lizzie said. She tucked Penny into bed. "I will be right back with your medicine."

"I don't want any medicine!" Penny shouted.

"You must have this medicine," Lizzie said when she came back. The wagon was filled with Lizzie's very own stuffed snake, Peter, her favorite King Kong picture, and a big orange. "See," Lizzie said. "I *can* be the big sister."

"You are a pretty good big sister after all." Penny hugged her sister.

"You are a pretty good big sister, too," said Lizzie.

"Thank you for giving me the *best* birthday present," said Penny. "Don't forget. Next week I will be *eight*. I can go to bed later than you. I will be very grown up. After all, I'm the *big* sister."

1. What did Lizzie and Penny decide about being a big sister?

2. Why did Penny want to be the little sister?

3. How did Lizzie try to act like a big sister?

4. How did you feel about Penny wanting to be the little sister?

5. When in the story did you begin to think that Penny was tired of playing the little sister?

Think and Write

Think about being the oldest, the youngest, or the only child in a family. Write about some of the special things you could do if you were the oldest, the youngest, or the only child.

Brother

by Mary Ann Hoberman

American Book Award Poet

I had a little brother
And I brought him to my mother
And I said I want another
Little brother for a change.
But she said don't be a bother
So I took him to my father
And I said this little bother
Of a brother's very strange.
But he said one little brother
Is exactly like another
And every little brother
Misbehaves a bit he said.
So I took the little bother
From my mother and my father
And I put the little bother
Of a brother back to bed.

•

Character

All stories and plays have characters. Characters are the people or animals in a story. In "Little Boss," the characters are Penny and Lizzie.

One way that authors tell us about characters is by what the characters say or do and how they say and do things.

Think about Penny in "Little Boss." She was upset because everyone was making a big fuss over Lizzie. The author tells us that Penny flopped down on the bed. The author used the word *flopped* because it helps you know Penny's mood. She is cross and upset. If the author had said that Penny sat down, or lay down, you would not know much about how she felt.

Authors choose words carefully to help readers know why the characters act and talk the way they do. Read the two paragraphs below. Think about how the author lets you know about the characters.

Karen went into the house. The door closed behind her. She put her things on the table and went to look for her dog. "Where are you, Spot?"

Karen stormed into the house. The door slammed behind her. She threw her things on the table and yelled, "Where are you, Spot?"

Which paragraph tells you the most about Karen? Which words help you to understand how Karen is feeling? The words *stormed, slammed, threw,* and *yelled* help you know how Karen feels.

As you read other stories, think about the words the author uses that help you to know the characters better.

John Newbery Honor Award Author

The Galumpagalooses

by Eloise Jarvis McGraw

*Jamie has some special homework.
What is Jamie supposed to do?
How does he do it?*

Jamie was given something special to do after school one day. His teacher, Ms. Morris, asked him to draw something no one had ever seen before. Jamie was excited, but he wasn't sure how to do this. When he got home, he told his mother what he was supposed to do. She told him to ask their friend, Mr. Rollo, for help. Mr. Rollo is an artist who lives in the same building as Jamie.

146

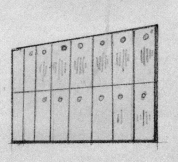

Jamie went to Mr. Rollo's door and knocked. Mr. Rollo opened the door. "Hi there, Jamie. How's it going?" asked Mr. Rollo.

"Mr. Rollo, you're an artist, aren't you?" asked Jamie.

"That's a fact," answered Mr. Rollo. "I'm certainly not anything else."

"A real artist?" asked Jamie.

"That's a different question," Mr. Rollo said, as he looked down at Jamie.

"Can you draw a picture of something that nobody's ever seen before?"

Mr. Rollo blinked and then said, "Certainly, I do that all the time."

"Really?" Jamie asked. He was excited. "You said that you only drew pictures of furniture and TV sets and . . ."

"That's at work. At home I draw things nobody's ever seen before." Mr. Rollo smiled at Jamie and said, "Come on in and see."

Jamie had never been in Mr. Rollo's home before. It wasn't what he expected. Mostly it was one long room, with some furniture way back in a corner and a strong smell of paint. There were pictures all over the walls. Jamie just stood and stared at the pictures—first one, then the next, then the next. All of the pictures were of things nobody had ever seen before.

"What are they, Mr. Rollo?" Jamie asked at last. "What do you call them?"

"Sometimes I call them abstractions. Sometimes I just call them shapes. Now and then I call one a galumpagaloos," Mr. Rollo answered.

Jamie laughed. He knew Mr. Rollo was joking. "But how do you draw an abstraction, or a galumpagaloos? How do you start?" he asked.

Mr. Rollo thought a minute, then said, "I look at something."

"Oh," said Jamie, not sure if that would help. "But it's supposed to be something nobody's ever seen."

"Nobody ever *has* seen it the way I see it, because nobody else is me. Look there, Jamie," said Mr. Rollo, turning Jamie to face a big painting on the wall. "Did you ever see the thing in that picture before?"

Jamie looked carefully. "No."

149

"As a matter of fact, you have," said Mr. Rollo. He turned Jamie to face the window. There was a bowl of flowers on the windowsill. Outside, Jamie could see a part of the library. "That's what you saw. I saw something nobody had ever seen before—not even me, until I drew it on the paper."

Jamie stared at the big painting, then at the window, and then at the big painting again. Slowly he began to understand. He felt very excited. He asked, "Could I draw one of those galumpagalooses, do you think?"

"I expect you could," said Mr. Rollo. "You'll never know till you try."

So Jamie tried. He hurried home and found some paper and a pencil. Then he looked at things. He looked until he really saw them in his very own way, and then he drew.

Right away he knew he was drawing
things he'd never seen before, until he
saw them on his paper. By the time his
mother came to look, Jamie had three sheets
of paper covered with drawings. When he
showed them to her, she said she'd
certainly never seen such things. Jamie
wasn't sure what Ms. Morris would say,
though.

The next morning at school, he took
all his pictures to Ms. Morris's desk.
She looked at him and then at the
papers in his hand. He handed her one
of his pictures. "Did you ever see that
thing before?"

Ms. Morris looked at it carefully. Then
she said, "No."

Jamie began to smile, because he knew she had, but not the way he had seen it. "It's a galumpagaloos," he said. He handed her his other drawings. "Here are eight more galumpagalooses."

Jamie watched Ms. Morris spread them out on her desk and stare at them, first one, then the next, then the next. Finally she looked up and said, "You did it."

"I told you I could do it," said Jamie. They grinned at each other.

1. What is Jamie supposed to do? How does he do it?

2. How did Mr. Rollo help Jamie "see" things in his own way?

3. How did Jamie solve his problem?

4. What did you think about Mr. Rollo's name for shapes or abstractions? Why?

5. When in the story did you first think Jamie would make Ms. Morris happy with his work?

Find something that you want to make a picture of and look at it closely. Make a picture of it. It can be an abstraction. Then write about the colors you used and how you felt about your work.

*In "The Galumpagalooses,"
Jamie drew things in his very
own way. Read to find out what
makes the art of Henri Matisse
so special.*

Henri Matisse, Artist

by Ruth Michaels

What would you think if you saw a grown man cutting things out of colored paper? Would you guess that this man was a famous artist? Well, he was. The man was Henri Matisse.

The Early Years

Henri Matisse was born in France in 1869. As a child, he didn't show any real interest in art. He studied law when he was a young man. Then one day, when he was sick, his mother brought him a box of paints to help him pass the time until he felt better.

Matisse started to paint by making
copies of famous paintings. He soon
found that he liked to paint so much
that he wanted to become an artist. He
decided to go to school and study art.
He also went to famous museums to
look at the paintings of other artists.

Matisse said, "For some time I painted
just like anyone else. But things didn't
go well at all, and I was unhappy.
Then, little by little, I began to paint
as I felt."

The Later Years

Matisse always kept trying new things. His art was different from that of other artists because of the way he used colors and shapes. Matisse said that when he wanted to paint a picture of fall, he did not try to copy just what he saw. Instead he painted the way fall made him feel. Matisse never painted sad things, because he wanted his art to make people feel happy.

Matisse became a very famous artist. People began to buy more and more of his paintings.

When Matisse was over seventy years old, he started using scissors and colored paper for his art. He cut out shapes and pasted these shapes on another piece of paper. Matisse called this "drawing with scissors." In the last four years of his life, Matisse did only cut-outs. He was not well, and this was the only work he could do. He didn't mind, though. When he was drawing with scissors, he said he was "cutting the colors out alive."

Matisse said that an artist has to look at life through the eyes of a child. By this he meant that an artist has to look at everything as if that artist were seeing it for the first time.

To some people, Matisse's artwork might seem like the work of a child. In fact, it could only have been done by a great artist. Today Matisse's paintings and his cut-outs are in museums all over the world.

1. What makes the art of Henri Matisse special?

2. How did Matisse use scissors to make art?

3. Do you like Matisse's art? Why or why not?

4. What did you read on page 157 that made you think that people liked Matisse's art?

5. Do you think you would enjoy being an artist? Explain your answer.

Think about the special kind of art that Henri Matisse did with scissors. Think about shapes and colors you like. Make your own "drawing with scissors" art. What do the colors and shapes make you think of? Write about your colors and shapes.

What is the mystery of Sara Beth? How does Becky solve it?

The Mystery of Sara Beth

by Polly Putnam

The mystery began in December. Becky and her friends were working. Wind and snow blew hard on the windows. The door opened, and a girl walked in and stood near the door. She wore a furry blue coat.

Miss Harris, the teacher, spoke to her. Then she said, "Class, this is our new girl. Her name is Sara Beth." Miss Harris pointed to the desk in front of Becky. "Sit there, Sara Beth."

Becky smiled when Sara Beth sat down, but Sara Beth didn't smile back. Sara Beth didn't turn around all morning. At noon Becky took Sara Beth to lunch. "Will you eat with us?" Becky asked. Sara Beth shook her head and went to a table by herself.

Becky and her friends sat at a table together. They talked about Sara Beth. "Why doesn't she want to make friends?" asked Becky.

"Maybe she is shy," said David.

"If we're nice to her, she'll soon be our friend," said Janie.

Becky, David, and Janie helped Sara Beth. Becky found some books for her. She gave Sara Beth a pencil and a ruler.

Sara Beth said, "Thank you," but she didn't smile, and she didn't talk any more.

Janie took Sara Beth to the gym. She
told Sara Beth the rules for the games.
Sara Beth said, "Thank you," but she
didn't say anything else.

David showed Sara Beth the library. He
helped Sara Beth take out a book. Sara
Beth said, "Thank you," but that was all.

"I give up," said Janie after a few days.
"Sara Beth doesn't want any friends."

"I want to know why," said Becky.
"Everyone wants friends."

Becky wanted to solve the mystery of why Sara Beth didn't want friends. She looked for clues.

Becky saw that Sara Beth's blue jeans were old and faded, but many children wore faded jeans. No, Sara Beth's clothes were not a clue to the mystery.

Becky had another idea. Maybe Sara Beth was afraid she couldn't do her schoolwork. Becky peeked at Sara Beth's papers. They said *Good* and had only a few red marks on them. Sara Beth often raised her hand to answer questions. She was on the same spelling page as Becky. No, Sara Beth wasn't worried about her schoolwork. Becky couldn't guess what was making Sara Beth so unfriendly.

163

Sara Beth stayed alone until the day Miss Harris put a big cage on the table. The children came up to the table and saw two guinea pigs. The children named the guinea pigs Harriet and Smitty.

"Someone will have to help feed and care for the guinea pigs every day," said Miss Harris. "Mondays and Thursdays the cage will have to be cleaned."

"I'll help," said Sara Beth. "I'll do it every Monday."

The next Monday Sara Beth cleaned the cage. She put down clean newspapers and hay. She filled the water bottle with fresh water, and she set out new food.

Then Sara Beth let Harriet and Smitty play on the table. She picked up Smitty and held him close while she petted him.

Becky was more puzzled than ever. Why would Sara Beth make friends with animals and not with her classmates?

During the next few days, three strange things happened. They gave Becky the clues she needed.

The first strange thing happened in the coatroom after school. Becky was alone with Sara Beth. A reading book dropped to the floor. Sara Beth had hidden it under her coat.

Becky said, "You know Miss Harris doesn't let us take reading books home. She's afraid they will be lost."

Sara Beth's face turned red. "Please don't tell," she said. Becky didn't tell, but she had her first clue.

The second strange thing happened during George's birthday party in school. He gave everyone a glass of punch and an apple. Sara Beth drank her punch, but she didn't eat her apple. She put it in her desk.

The third strange thing happened on a Thursday. It was Janie's day to clean the guinea pig cage. While Janie was cleaning the cage, Harriet jumped off the table. She ran all around under the desks. All the children tried to catch her. Everyone was laughing and shouting.

Becky was the only one watching Sara Beth. Sara Beth wasn't chasing Harriet. Sara Beth was standing on a chair. Her face was white, and she was shaking. She was afraid! Becky had her third clue. It was the strangest of all.

Becky thought about the three clues.

1. Sara Beth broke the rule about
   taking a reading book home.
2. Sara Beth saved her apple instead of
   eating it.
3. Sometimes Sara Beth loved guinea
   pigs, and sometimes she was afraid
   of them.

All at once Becky solved the mystery!
She knew why Sara Beth would not make
any friends.

Becky could hardly wait for the chance to see Sara Beth alone. During art Miss Harris said, "Becky and Sara Beth, please go to the art room to get more paint."

In the art room, Sara Beth reached for a jar of paint. "Tell me," said Becky. "Are you Sara, or are you Beth?"

Sara Beth almost dropped the paint. "What do you mean?" she asked.

"I know you're a twin," said Becky, "and I know you take turns coming to school."

Sara Beth's eyes opened wide. "It's true," she said. "How did you know?"

Becky said, "You gave me some clues. I guessed that the reading book and the apple were going home to someone. I didn't know who until today, when you jumped up in the chair. You are afraid of Harriet. Your twin is not."

Sara Beth sat down. "I'm Beth," she said. "Now I have given away the secret." Beth put her head in her hands. Becky put her arm around Beth.

"You were both unfriendly so no one would find out your secret," said Becky.

"Yes," said Beth.

"I don't understand," said Becky. "Why couldn't you both come to school?"

"We have just moved from a place where the weather is not so cold," said Beth. "We have only one warm coat. Sara and I take turns wearing it."

Becky said, "After school we'll tell Miss Harris. She'll know what to do."

"I'm afraid she'll be angry," said Beth.

Miss Harris wasn't angry. "We'll look in the office, Beth," she said. "There are extra hats. Maybe there is an extra coat."

Beth looked surprised. "You mean there are other children without warm clothes?" she asked.

Miss Harris smiled. "Certainly."

The next day two smiling girls walked into Becky's classroom. One was wearing a furry blue coat. The other was wearing a brown coat.

Now Becky had a new mystery to solve. Which twin was Sara, and which was Beth?

1. What was the mystery of Sara Beth?

2. What three clues did Becky use to solve the mystery?

3. How was the mystery resolved?

4. Do you think Sara and Beth had a good plan for going to school? Why do you think that?

5. When in the story did you know that Becky was sure there was a mystery about Sara Beth?

6. How did Becky discover the clues that helped her solve the mystery?

Think and Write

Pretend that you have a twin. Your twin is just like you. Make up a name for your twin. Write about what your twin is like. Share your writing with a friend.

Reader Awareness

Do you ever think about why you read something? When you began to read "The Mystery of Sara Beth," were you thinking that you wanted to find out what the mystery was? If so, that was your **purpose,** or reason, for reading.

When you read a mystery, you know that there will be a problem to solve. You need to think about how clues are put together to solve the mystery.

As you were reading the story, you might have had new purposes. Read the paragraphs below.

Becky said, "After school we'll tell Miss Harris. She'll know what to do."

"I'm afraid she'll be angry," said Beth.

Would Miss Harris be angry? You may have thought that she would not be angry, but you couldn't be sure until you read on. You read on with a purpose.

What if you want to build a birdhouse? You have a book of plans. Will your purpose for reading be the same as when you read a story? Read the paragraph below.

Read all the directions first. Be sure you have enough wood and the right tools before you begin. Use your tools safely. Ask your mother or father to help you.

What is your purpose for reading? You want to find out how to do something. When you read for information or to learn about something, you may read more slowly. You may need to read some parts again to be sure you understand.

Before you read something, think about your purpose, or reason, for reading. As you read, ask yourself: What am I learning?

*You don't always need words to
talk. What are some ways you
can talk without words?*

Talking Without Words

Story and pictures by Marie Hall Ets

"Give me some of your peanuts," says
Bear, but he doesn't say it in words. He
just opens his mouth and holds up his
paw.

"I want to see *them* without their seeing
me," says Sister, but not in words. She
just hides behind the house and peeks.

"I love the smell of flowers!" says Little
Brother, but he doesn't say it in words.
He just runs and smells the flowers
whenever he sees some.

"Come here. I have something nice for you," says Mother to Little Brother, but not in words. She just motions to him.

When I'm too hot, I take off my coat. When Sister's too cold, she hugs herself and shivers. We don't need to use words to say so.

"Throw it to me, too!" says Little Brother
when Big Brother and Sister are playing
ball. He just says it with his hands.

"I don't want to hear!" says Little
Brother when Mother starts scolding. He
doesn't say it in words. He just covers
his ears.

"Don't wake the baby," says Mother, but without using words. She just motions by putting a finger on her lips and Little Brother understands.

"Good-bye!" I wave as you go away. You are too far for words, so I only hope you'll turn around and wave good-bye to me.

1. How can you talk without words?

2. Tell four things that were said without words. How were they said?

3. Which of the ways of talking without words do you use most?

4. When was it easiest for you to tell what was being said from looking at the picture?

5. When was it hardest for you to tell what was being said from looking at the picture?

Drawing pictures can be a way of telling a story without words. Think about something that has happened to you or is important to you. Tell your story by drawing pictures. Under each picture write what is happening.

Whistling

by Jack Prelutsky

Oh, I can laugh and I can sing
and I can scream and shout,
but when I try to whistle,
the whistle won't come out.

I shape my lips the proper way,
I make them small and round,
but when I blow, just air comes out,
there is no whistling sound.

But I'll keep trying very hard
to whistle loud and clear,
and someday soon I'll whistle tunes
for everyone to hear.

181

Coretta Scott King Award Author

Sammy and Jacob are good friends.
How do they help each other?

My Friend Jacob

by Lucille Clifton

My best friend lives next door. His
name is Jacob. He is my very, very best
friend.

We do things together, Jacob and me.
We love to play basketball together. Jacob
always makes a basket on the first try.
He helps me to learn how to hold the
ball so that I can make baskets, too.

My mother used to say, "Be careful
with Jacob and that ball. He might hurt
you." Now she knows that Jacob
wouldn't hurt anybody, especially his
very, very best friend.

I love to sit on the steps for hours and
watch the cars go by with Jacob. He
knows the name of every kind of car.
Even if he only sees it just for a minute,
Jacob can tell you the kind of car.

Jacob is helping me learn to name the
cars, too. When I make a mistake, Jacob
never ever laughs. He just says, "No,
no, Sam. Try again." Then I do. He is
my best, best friend.

When I have to go to the store, Jacob goes with me to help. His mother used to say, "You don't have to have Jacob tagging along with you like that, Sammy." Now she knows we like to go to the store together. Jacob helps me to carry, and I help Jacob to remember.

"Red is for stop," I say if Jacob forgets. "Green is for go."

"Thank you, Sam," Jacob always says.

Jacob's birthday and my birthday are two days apart. Sometimes we celebrate together. Last year he made me a surprise. He had been having a secret for weeks and weeks, and my mother knew, and his mother knew, but they wouldn't tell me.

Jacob would stay in his house for an
hour every afternoon and not say
anything to me when he came out. He
would just smile and smile.

On my birthday, my mother made a
cake especially for me with eight candles.
Jacob's mother made a cake especially for
him with seventeen candles. We sat on
the porch and sang and blew out our
candles. Jacob blew out all seventeen
candles in one breath because he's bigger.

Then my mother smiled, and Jacob's mother smiled and said, "Give it to him, Jacob dear." My friend Jacob smiled and handed me a card.

HAPPY BIRTHDAY SAM
JACOB

He had printed it all by himself! All by himself, he printed my name and everything! It was neat!

My very best friend Jacob does so much to help me, I wanted to help him, too. One day I decided to teach him how to knock before he comes into my house.

Jacob would just walk into people's houses if he knew them. If he didn't know them, he would stand on the porch until somebody noticed him and let him in. "I wish Jacob would knock on the door," I heard my mother say.

I decided to help him learn. Every day I would tell Jacob, but he would always forget. He would just open the door and walk right in. My mother said maybe it was too hard for him and I shouldn't worry about it. I felt bad because Jacob always helped me so much, and I wanted to be able to help him, too.

I kept telling him and he kept forgetting, so one day I just said, "Never mind, Jacob, maybe it is too hard."

"What's the matter, Sam?" Jacob asked me.

"Never mind, Jacob," was all I said.

Next day we were sitting in our dining room when my mother and my father and I heard this really loud knocking at the door. Then the door popped open and Jacob stuck his head in. "I'm knocking, Sam!" he yelled.

Boy, I jumped right up from the table and grinned and hugged Jacob. He grinned and hugged me, too. He is my very, very, very best friend in the whole wide world!

1. How did Sam and Jacob help each other?

2. What special thing did Sam do for Jacob, and how did he do it?

3. How did you feel when Jacob knocked on Sam's door? Why?

4. When did you know that Jacob had trouble learning some things?

5. When did you know that Jacob could learn new things?

Think and Write

Think about what a special friend has done to help you. Write a short thank-you note to your friend. Make sure your friend knows how important his or her help was to you.

Thinking About "Bridges"

In this unit you learned that people have different ways of building bridges to others. Sometimes a bridge is built when two people try to understand each other.

Penny and Lizzie traded places and built a bridge of understanding. Mr. Rollo helped Jamie to see things in a new way. Matisse reached out to all of us with his paintings and cut-outs.

Sara and Beth needed the bridge of friendship and found it with Becky and their classmates. Jacob and Sam had a special bridge between them.

As you read other stories, think about the problems people have when there is no bridge of understanding. Then think about the bridges that people build to reach each other.

1. How are the stories "Little Boss" and "The Mystery of Sara Beth" the same? How are they different?

2. Do you think that Mr. Rollo from "The Galumpagalooses" would have liked to meet Matisse? Why?

3. How is the friendship of Jamie and Mr. Rollo like that of Sammy and Jacob? How is it different?

4. Which person in this unit do you think did the best job of building a bridge of understanding? Why?

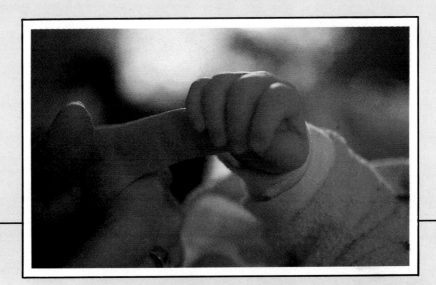

Patterns

A pattern is something that we see over and over. In "Patterns," you will read some stories that were first told long ago. They have been told over and over. Your parents and grandparents may have read or heard these stories.

Some of these stories tell about the patterns of life in the past. Others teach lessons that have been taught over and over. Some compare life in one place with life in another. Some compare life in different seasons.

As you read, think about why these stories are in a unit called "Patterns."

Read on Your Own

Little Nino's Pizzeria *by Karen Barbour. Harcourt Brace Jovanovich.* Little Tony and his family are happy with the little pizzeria, but success leads to a bigger restaurant where Tony is only in the way.

Dog for a Day *by Dick Gackenbach. Clarion.* Second-grader Sidney invents a Changing Box and changes places with his dog. It seems like fun until he sees how hard it is to be a dog.

Bread and Jam for Frances *by Russell Hoban. Harper.* Frances Badger decides she will eat only bread and jam, but her parents are too helpful, and Frances decides enough is enough.

Harry's Visit *by Barbara Ann Porte. Greenwillow.* Harry does not want to visit his father's friends, but he discovers that other families can be both different and fun.

I Wish Laura's Mommy Was My Mommy
by Barbara Power. Lippincott. Jennifer's
mother works, and there are other
children in the family. Laura is an only
child, and her mother is home all day.
Everything seems better at Laura's house
until the situation changes, and the two
homes are not so different after all.

Henry and Mudge in Puddle Trouble *by
Cynthia Rylant. Bradbury.* Henry and
his dog Mudge have fun together in the
spring. Dad finds it can be fun acting
like a kid for a while.

The Story of Bentley Beaver *by Marjorie
Weinman Sharmat. Harper.* Bentley Beaver
builds with wood and builds
his life. We meet his children and
grandchildren.

This is an old tale that has been told over and over again. What does Country Mouse learn from his visit to the city?

City Mouse and Country Mouse

An Aesop fable retold by Jane Lawrence

Once, in a field of tall grass, there lived a small mouse. He was quite happy with his life, all in all. He had a snug place to sleep where he was safe. He had plenty of food to eat, too. From here and there he picked up crumbs and vegetables. On good days he might even find some dry cheese.

Yes, indeed. Country Mouse had a good life and was very happy.

One day, as he leaned back on a
small pile of grass, he wondered
whatever had happened to his cousin,
City Mouse. He wrote a letter asking
City Mouse how he was and if he'd like
to come for a visit to the country.

For a long time Country Mouse didn't
hear anything from his cousin. He
almost forgot about the letter. Then one
day, who should turn up in his field
but his cousin, City Mouse.

The two mice were very glad to see
each other. They talked and talked all
afternoon about this and that, catching
up on all the news.

For dinner Country Mouse went out to get all the best bits of food he could find. He wanted to serve an extra-nice meal on this happy day.

As City Mouse was wiping his mouth after dinner, he said, "Well, that was not bad, cousin. It was not bad, but not good either. How can you stand to live this way?"

"What do you mean?" asked Country Mouse. "Live what way?"

City Mouse sniffed, and smoothed his whiskers with great care. "Well," he said, "it's just so dull here. There is nothing to do, no one to see, no place to go. I can't believe your food! What can I say?"

"What's wrong with my food?" asked Country Mouse, his feelings hurt. After all, he had worked very hard to fix a good dinner. "Didn't you get plenty to eat?"

"Oh, I got plenty," said City Mouse. "But, cousin, it was not my idea of good. It was plain and dull."

Country Mouse's face grew sad. "I'm sorry you didn't like it," he said, trying not to let his hurt feelings show.

"I guess there isn't anything you can do about it," said City Mouse. "Out here in the country, you just don't have much to pick from."

"I did the very best I could," said Country Mouse in a small voice.

"Of course you did," said City Mouse. "Now, I have a great idea. You can come back to the city with me. There are things to do, places to go. Wait until you taste the food I will serve!"

The two cousins set off for the city. Soon they were at City Mouse's house. It was everything City Mouse had said it would be.

The rugs were beautiful bright colors. In each room were beautiful chairs and tables and lights. Best of all was the kitchen. Country Mouse ran up and down everywhere. Everything in the kitchen was shining and bright. There, right in front of his eyes, was a mountain of food.

Never in his whole life had he seen such food. "May I have some of it?" Country Mouse asked City Mouse.

"Of course you may," answered City Mouse. "What do you think I've been telling you? This is the best place in the whole world to live."

So Country Mouse ate and ate. He had never eaten such food. He thought he might never be so happy again. "The city is the place for me," he said. "Do you eat like this every day?"

"But of course!" said City Mouse. "This is the city! We live very well here." City Mouse sniffed, and smoothed his whiskers, the way he did when he was pleased with himself.

Just then came a loud banging and thumping noise down the hall. Country Mouse was just getting ready to take one more large bite of cheese, but he stopped cold.

"What is that?" he asked, and looked over at City Mouse.

"Tell you later," City Mouse panted. He grabbed Country Mouse's paw and pulled him hard. "Run for your life!"

They ran, slipping and sliding, as the noise got closer and closer. At last they were safe behind some cups on a high shelf. Country Mouse took a deep breath.

"What was that all about?" he asked.

"It was the house animals," answered City Mouse. "When they come into the kitchen, we have to run, or they'll get us."

"Is it like this every day?" asked Country Mouse.

"Every day," answered City Mouse.
"You get used to it after a while,
though."

"Not me," said Country Mouse. "I
don't want to get used to it." As soon
as the house animals went away,
Country Mouse jumped down and
headed for the kitchen door.

"Where are you going?" shouted City
Mouse. "I have much more to show
you!"

"Not me," said Country Mouse over
his shoulder. "I don't need to see
anything else. I'm going back to the
country right now."

"But there isn't anything to do
there," said City Mouse. "You'll never
eat the way you ate here tonight."

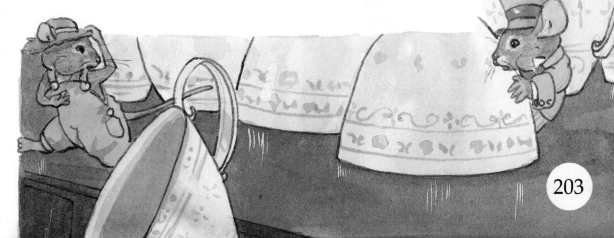

"Maybe I won't," said Country Mouse. "On the other hand, I'll never be eaten either, and I don't have to be afraid. I can eat my plain food without having to worry about someone coming to get me. So long, City Mouse. I hope I can see you again some day. Come visit me again, if you are able."

Country Mouse ran all the way back to his home in the country as fast as his little legs would carry him. He lived a long and happy life, even if he didn't have such an exciting life.

Remember: Be happy with what you have.

1. What did Country Mouse learn?

2. Why did City Mouse ask Country Mouse to come to the city?

3. Why did Country Mouse run away from the city?

4. How do you feel about Country Mouse returning to the country? What else could he have done?

5. When in the story did you first think that Country Mouse might not want to stay in the city?

Pretend that you are a city mouse. You are trying to decide whether you should move to the country or stay in the city. On one side of your paper, write all the reasons to stay in the city. On the other side, write reasons to move to the country. Then write what you decide to do.

Rudolph Is Tired of the City

by Gwendolyn Brooks

These buildings are too close to me.
I'd like to *push* away.
I'd like to live in the country,
And spread my arms all day.

I'd like to spread my breath out, too—
As farmers' sons and daughters do.

I'd tend the cows and chickens.
I'd do the other chores.
Then, all the hours left I'd go
A-spreading out-of-doors.

The boy in this story has one grandfather who lives in the city and one who lives in the country. What does the boy learn from each grandfather?

City Grandfather, Country Grandfather

by Robert Hasselblad

I have two grandfathers. One lives in the city. One lives in the country.

My city grandfather lives on a wide street, lined with houses. In front of his house are a sidewalk, a streetlight, and a small yard.

My country grandfather lives at the end of a dirt road. In front of his house are a large gate, an apple tree, and a big yard.

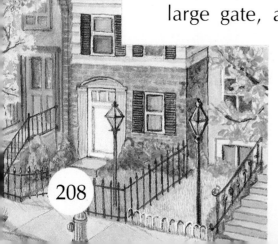

208

My city grandfather works in an office.
He rides up to his office in an elevator.
He is a businessman.

My country grandfather works in his
fields and barn. He rides on a big green
tractor. He is a farmer.

My city grandfather has a big desk with
a telephone on it. He talks to many people
on the telephone every day. He also has
an adding machine in his office. He adds
lots of numbers on it. The answers come
out on a long roll of paper.

My country grandfather has many cows
that he milks each day. He has machines
that do this. He stores the milk until a
truck comes to collect it.

When I visit my city grandfather at his office, he lets me add numbers on the adding machine. I lick stamps for his letters. We take the mail to the mail drop near the elevator. He tells me that I am learning about business.

When I visit my country grandfather, he lets me pet the cows to keep them happy. He lets me ride with him on the tractor. We go to the mailbox at the end of the road. He tells me that I am learning about farming.

My city grandfather drives a shiny blue car. Sometimes he drives to other cities on business.

My country grandfather drives an old red truck. Sometimes he drives to town to get things he needs.

When I visit my city grandfather, we ride our bikes together all around town. We buy popcorn to feed the birds in the park.

When I visit my country grandfather, we build a fire. Then we sing songs.

At the end of every visit, both my city grandfather and my country grandfather do exactly the same thing. They both give me big bear hugs and say, "See you real soon!" Maybe when I grow up, I'll be a farmer and live in the country. Maybe I'll be a businessman and live in the city. I know about both.

1. What does the boy learn from each grandfather?

2. In what ways are the grandfathers alike?

3. What did you like best about each grandfather?

4. Find the words that tell how the grandfathers feel about the boy.

5. Compare the patterns of the lives of the two grandfathers.

6. Are the country grandfather's feelings about the boy different from the city grandfather's feelings? Explain your answer.

Pretend you are going to visit one of the grandfathers or some other special person. Write a story telling who you would like to visit and why. Tell what you would like to do during your visit.

Compare and Contrast

Think about City Mouse and Country Mouse. How are they the same? Did you remember that they are both mice? Did you say that they are both afraid of the house animals? Did you remember that they both like good food?

When you think about how two things are alike you **compare** them.

Now think about how City Mouse and Country Mouse are different. One likes the city. The other likes the country. One likes plain food and a safe life. The other likes fancy food and an exciting life.

When you think about how things are different, you **contrast** them.

Sometimes an author compares or contrasts by using clue words such as *both, they,* or *but.* Look for clue words as you read the paragraph below.

Susan and Donna both like to iceskate. Both girls have new skates. In the wintertime, they skate every weekend. Susan can do tricks on her skates, but Donna is still having a hard time just standing up.

Did you find the clue words the author used to compare the girls? The clue words were *both* and *they.* Did you find three ways the girls were alike?

What clue word told you the author was contrasting the two girls? The word *but* in the last sentence told you that there was a difference between the girls.

As you read, look for clue words that the author uses to help you see the comparisons or contrasts that are being made.

Like "Country Mouse and City Mouse," this is an old tale. What does the ant in this story teach the grasshopper?

The Ant and the Grasshopper

An Aesop fable retold by M. Drummond

It was summertime. Every day the grasshopper fiddled and sang. He didn't worry about anything at all. He loved the excitement of summer.

Every day the ant worked very hard gathering food. Then he carried it to a safe place.

"Why do you work so hard?" the grasshopper asked the ant.

"I work because winter is coming," said the ant.

"Winter is a long way off," said the grasshopper. "Come and dance."

"I can't," said the ant. "I told you, winter is coming."

"Well, it is summer now," said the grasshopper. "Now is the time to fiddle and sing. Feel that nice hot sun. Look at the nice green grass. Smell the beautiful flowers."

The ant sighed. "I'd like to dance and fiddle and sing with you," he said. "Perhaps when my work is done I can."

At that the grasshopper laughed. "You'll never be done. You just run around gathering food and carrying it from one place to the other all day. You miss all the excitement in life."

The ant gave a small smile. "I know it may seem that I am missing the excitement, but wait and see. When winter comes, I'll be thankful that I worked so hard."

"Well, that's not the life for me," said the grasshopper. "I can't think about winter now. When it gets here, I'll think about it."

All summer long it was the same. Every day the grasshopper fiddled and sang. Every day the grasshopper tried to talk the ant into singing and dancing with him. Every day the ant said he didn't have time. Every day the ant worked harder and harder, gathering and storing up food.

Then the days began to change. The leaves on the trees turned different colors. The flowers began to dry up. Pretty soon cold winds began to blow, and the sun was not so warm in the daytime. The nights got colder and colder, and snow began to fall.

The ant kept warm in his anthill. When he was hungry, he ate the food he had stored up from the summer.

The grasshopper hopped all over looking for something to eat. There was nothing to be found anywhere. He got thinner and thinner. He was very tired, he was very cold, and he was very hungry.

At last the grasshopper knew he could not last another day. He went to the ant and said, "Please give me some food. Just a bite would be nice. I am so very hungry. I can't find anything to eat, and you have so much."

"I'm very sorry," said the ant, for he
was a kind ant. "I really wish I could
help you, but I can't. I have only enough
food for myself and my family."

"I shouldn't have played and sung all
summer," sighed the grasshopper. "I
should have gathered and stored up food
the way you did." The grasshopper pulled
his wings close around him and walked
sadly away into the wind and cold.

The hardworking ant could have said, "I told you so." He was a kind ant, though, so he didn't say anything at all. He just shook his head and watched the grasshopper walk away.

Remember: Save while you can. You may not have a chance later.

1. What did the ant teach the grasshopper?

2. Why did the ant work hard all summer?

3. How was the problem resolved, and how is this story different from most stories you have read?

4. How did you feel about the ant not sharing his food with the grasshopper?

5. Where in the story did you learn that the grasshopper never worked?

The ant remembered "Save while you can." Think about different ways that people save. Write about your ideas on saving. Share with a friend.

Any Me
I Want to Be

by Karla Kuskin

All my legs were very tired.
I had walked, I think, forever
When I came upon a mountain
Wide and high as any mountain
Standing quite alone.
"That's no mountain,"
Said my mother.
"That is just a stone."

We walked on
Me and my mother
Past a dragon that was not
A dragon
But a caterpillar.
Past a very little pot
With some water in the bottom.
"Look," I said, "a lake."
"You are small," my mother told me.
"And you make a small mistake."

All my feet were very weary
I looked up to see the sky
And I saw a tree above me
Tall and leafy
Green and high.
"That's no tree," my mother told me.
"That is just a plant.
It is leafy green and little.
It looks tall
Because you're smaller
Than most things are,"
Said my mother.
Mother is an ant.

Did you know that there is more than one kind of squirrel? Read to find out how the gray squirrel and the ground squirrel are the same. How are they different?

Squirrels in Winter

by Ruth Michaels

Gray Squirrel

The gray squirrel is hungry. It comes down from its nest high up in a tree to look for food. As the squirrel runs along the ground, it sees a flower. The flower looks very good, so the squirrel stops to have a bite to eat. The squirrel turns the flower in its paws as it takes small bites. A flower isn't what the squirrel really wants, though.

The gray squirrel is really searching for nuts. That's what the gray squirrel likes best of all. It finds a nut. The nut tastes very good. The squirrel holds the nut in its paws, cracks the shell, and eats the nut meat.

Soon the squirrel finds another nut. This nut is starting to grow roots and would not be good to eat. The squirrel puts this nut back into the earth where it can keep growing. Someday the nut will be a fine tall tree.

Winter is coming soon. The gray squirrel will spend most of the winter in its nest high up in a tree. Every three or four days it will leave its warm nest to look for food. Down the tree the squirrel will go, looking for nuts stored in the ground.

During the summer, the gray squirrel had found many nuts and put them into the ground. It dug holes about three inches deep, one for each nut. It dropped each nut into a hole and then pushed the dirt back to cover it up. During the winter, the squirrel comes back to these holes for food.

How does the gray squirrel know where to find the nuts that were put into the ground earlier? The squirrel doesn't have to remember. Its nose does the work. Once the nut is found, the squirrel smells the nut to see if it is a good one. If the nut is good, the squirrel eats fast and hurries back home to its nest in the tree.

The gray squirrel is much safer in a tree than it is on the ground.

Ground Squirrel

The ground squirrel worries about winter. It also worries about summer. This squirrel can live almost anywhere, but it doesn't like very hot or very cold weather.

The ground squirrel lives beneath the ground. It digs a home so that it is safely hidden from other animals that might want to harm it. This squirrel also digs a storeroom for its food.

During the spring, the ground squirrel eats a lot of food and gets very fat. Because of all this fat, it can go for a long time without eating. When the very hot weather comes, the ground squirrel goes into its home beneath the ground and stays there. It waits for cooler weather.

As soon as the weather gets cooler, the ground squirrel comes out from beneath the ground. Again it begins to gather food. This time the ground squirrel is getting ready for winter. The squirrel looks for nuts. It stuffs the nuts into a special pouch in its mouth and carries the nuts to its underground storeroom. It fills the storeroom with good food.

By the first snow of winter, the ground squirrel has grown very fat again. It hurries beneath the ground to its safe home. Then it curls up in a ball and goes to sleep. Sometimes it wakes up, but it doesn't need to go out for food. The food is right there in the storeroom. The ground squirrel doesn't even know about the wind and snow outside.

There are many other kinds of squirrels besides the gray squirrel and the ground squirrel. Even though the squirrels are different in some ways, they are all the same in two ways. All squirrels need safe places to live and food for the winter.

1. How are the two kinds of squirrels the same? How are they different?

2. Where do gray squirrels live? Where do ground squirrels live?

3. What do both kinds of squirrels do to get ready for winter?

4. Which kind of squirrel do you think is safer in winter?

5. What did you read that made you think that a gray squirrel has a good sense of smell?

**Think
and
Write**

Animals get ready for winter in different ways. Choose an animal and find out what it does to prepare for winter. Write about what you have learned.

Who is Betsy Ross? How did she use a needle to "fight for freedom"?

A Needle Fights for Freedom

by Esther MacLellan and Catherine V. Schroll

CHARACTERS

Peggy	**Mistress Betsy Ross**
Constance	**General Washington**
Elizabeth	**Robert Morris**
Anne	**Colonel Jones**
Prue	

Time: June 1776

Setting: Betsy Ross's home in Philadelphia. Girls are seated in a circle, sewing.

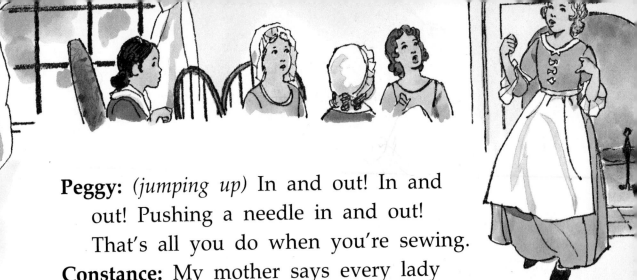

Peggy: *(jumping up)* In and out! In and out! Pushing a needle in and out! That's all you do when you're sewing.

Constance: My mother says every lady should be able to sew.

Elizabeth: So does mine.

Anne: There! I've stuck my finger again! Mean old needle!

Prue: My grandmother says we should be glad that Mistress Betsy Ross is teaching us to sew.

Peggy: Well, I'm not glad. I wish I were a boy. I'd join the army.

Prue: You're not big enough.

Peggy: I'm big enough to play a drum. *(pretends to beat a drum)* I'd be helping my country, too. How can you fight for freedom with a needle? *(Betsy Ross comes in.)*

Betsy Ross: Maybe you can't fight with a needle, Peggy, and maybe you can.

Peggy: Fight with a needle? How would a needle help our soldiers?

Betsy Ross: A needle makes warm clothes for the soldiers.

Peggy: I'm just sewing an old seam. I can't make clothes.

Betsy Ross: You never will be able to make clothes until you first learn on small things. Now show me your work. (*walks around the circle as she speaks*) Very nice, Prue. A little crooked, Anne. Peggy, your stitches are much too large.

Peggy: I wish they were even larger. Then I'd be finished.

Betsy Ross: Now you must rip out your seam and do it over.

Peggy: Again?

Betsy Ross: Again and again, until it's right. (*She leaves.*)

Constance: That's too bad, Peggy.

Peggy: *(sighing)* Well, I did hurry. If I were only helping in the fight for freedom, instead of just sewing! How I would love to do something for General Washington, something he really needed. *(sound of knocking is heard)*

Prue: Shall I answer the door?

Anne: Why not? Mistress Ross is busy in the kitchen. *(Prue goes to the door. General Washington, Robert Morris, and Colonel Jones come in.)*

Washington: Is this the home of Mistress Betsy Ross?

Prue: *(curtsying)* Yes, sir.

Peggy: *(rising)* Anne! Anne! That's General Washington!

Anne: You must be wrong, Peggy.

Peggy: Indeed I am not! *(to Washington)* Oh, sir, you *are* General Washington, aren't you?

Washington: *(bowing)* I am, indeed. *(Other men sit.)*

Peggy: But what are you doing *here*, sir? I thought you were busy.

Washington: *(smiling)* I *am* busy.

Peggy: I'm sorry, sir, I didn't mean you weren't. I meant busy in the army.

Washington: Not all the time, my dear.

Mr. Morris: Where is Mistress Ross?

Constance: I'll get her, sir. *(leaves)*

Mr. Morris: *(to Washington)* Are you sure that Mistress Ross will be able to do what we want?

Washington: I've heard that she is a fine needlewoman.

Elizabeth: Yes, sir, she is. Mistress Ross sews better than anyone else in Philadelphia.

Colonel Jones: Then she's the lady we want to meet. *(Betsy Ross comes in, followed by Constance.)*

Betsy Ross: *(curtsying)* General Washington! What a wonderful surprise, sir. What can I do for you?

Washington: Mistress Ross, this is Mr. Robert Morris and Colonel Jones.

Mr. Morris: *(bowing)* A pleasure, Mistress Ross.

Colonel Jones: *(bowing)* A pleasure.

Washington: We have come to ask you to do something important for your country.

Peggy: Is Mistress Ross to fight, sir?

Elizabeth: Peggy, do be quiet. General Washington will be angry.

Washington: Angry? Not I. There are other ways to help one's country. Mistress Ross can help us with her needle.

Colonel Jones: Mistress Ross, our country needs a flag.

Mr. Morris: Now that we are fighting England, we can no longer use the English flag that we once loved.

Colonel Jones: The colonies must have a flag of their own.

Washington: We need *one* flag for everybody. Then people will know that they are part of a new country.

Mr. Morris: They will know this is a free country, too, General Washington. All the colonies will be joined together under one great flag.

Betsy Ross: I shall do my best

Washington: I am sure of it. These are our plans. *(takes paper from his pocket)* What do you think of this?

Betsy Ross: It's beautiful, General Washington. I like the thirteen stripes and thirteen stars.

Mr. Morris: Yes, a stripe and a star for each of the thirteen colonies.

Betsy Ross: (*pointing to plan*) This is the six-pointed star of the English flag. Let's have a new star for our new country. What do you say to a five-pointed star?

Washington: Would it be very hard to make?

Betsy Ross: Not at all, sir. Peggy, hand me your sewing, my child. *(pretends to cut and hold up a star)* How do you like the star, General Washington?

Washington: *(rising)* Very much. Mistress Ross, we will leave the plan with you.

Betsy Ross: I shall start at once.

Washington: Good!

Mr. Morris: Work fast, Mistress Ross. Our country needs its flag.

Washington: It does, indeed. Good-bye, Mistress Ross. *(to girls)* Good-bye, my dears. If you learn to sew as well as your good teacher, maybe one day your needles may help our country, too.

Betsy Ross: *(curtsying)* Good-bye, sir. *(The three men leave.)*

Peggy: To think my ugly old sewing would be the first star of our new flag!

Constance: (*waving her sewing*) I say that the needle that makes a flag is a needle that fights for freedom!

Peggy: (*slowly*) Well, I suppose you're right, Constance, though I still wish I could beat a drum. (*throws arms around Betsy Ross*) Even if I'm not very good at sewing, I'm very proud of my teacher.

Betsy Ross: Thank you, Peggy. Sewing class is over, girls. This very minute, I must start to make our first American flag!

Discuss the Selection

1. Who is Betsy Ross and how did she use a needle to "fight for freedom"?

2. Why did General Washington want a new flag?

3. Which character in this play would you most like to be? Why?

4. Find the words that tell how Peggy felt about the fight for freedom.

5. Who were the people who helped in this play? How did they help?

Think and Write

Pretend that you are in the room when George Washington enters. This is a special day that you don't want to forget. Write down the date and what you want to remember about General Washington's visit.

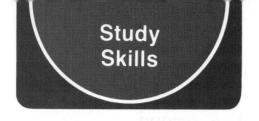

Follow Directions

Make a Star Mobile

In "A Needle Fights for Freedom," Betsy Ross was asked to use a plan to make a new flag for America. Sometimes you may make something from a plan, too. Often there are written directions to follow. These directions may have two or more steps.

When you are going to follow written directions, here are some things you should do.

1. Gather everything you need.
2. Read through all the steps. Then read them again.
3. Be sure you understand each step.
4. Follow each step in order.

Listed below are directions for making a star mobile. The first set of directions tells how to make the stars. The second set of directions tells how to put the stars together to make a mobile.

To Make the Stars

Things you will need: paper, pencil, scissors

1. On a piece of paper, draw a star to use as a pattern.

2. Cut out the pattern.

3. On another piece of paper, trace the pattern eight times.

4. Cut out the eight stars. This will give you four pairs of stars.

To Make the Mobile

Things you will need: stars, scissors, enough yarn for four ten-inch pieces, glue, coat hanger

1. Cut four pieces of yarn, one piece for each pair of stars. Each piece of yarn should be ten inches long.

2. Lay one star from each pair on the table.

3. Glue a piece of yarn to each star on the table.

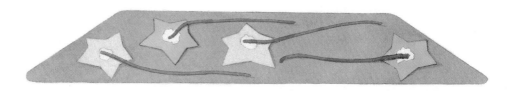

4. Take the second star of each pair and put it on top of the first star, yarn, and glue. You have glued the two stars together. Do this for each star pair. When you have finished, you will have four star pairs.

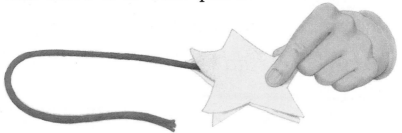

5. Tie the other end of each piece of yarn to the coat hanger. You may wish to tie the yarn so that some pieces are shorter than others.

You have made a star mobile!

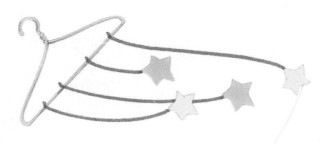

Like Betsy Ross, Mary McDonald helped her country in a very special way during the Revolutionary War. What did Mary do?

Thanks to Mary

by Ann Bixby Herold

Mary McDonald was a young girl during the Revolutionary War. She worried about the hungry soldiers with General Washington at Valley Forge. Mary worked in a big house where there was lots of food. She began to think of what she could do to help the soldiers.

Every time Mary sat down to eat, she
thought about the soldiers. She had
plenty to eat, and they were hungry.
She had warm clothes to wear, and
they were cold. It worried her more
and more.

She started to save some of her food—
some nuts here, an apple there. Then
she took the food she had saved to
General Washington's tent. "I'm Mary
McDonald. I've come to join the army,"
she told the soldier standing there.

"You? Girls can't join the army."

"I've brought some food," said Mary, as she handed him an apple.

The soldier smiled down at her. "Follow me, miss," he said. He took her to Mrs. Washington. "Mary McDonald is here to join the army, ma'am," he said.

Mrs. Washington smiled at Mary. "We have need of busy hands," she said.

There was plenty of work for Mary to do. She sewed. She knitted. She carried baskets of food to the sick soldiers.

Mary also ran messages. No one ever stopped or questioned her. She could carry messages to places a grown-up could not go.

Hurrying along an icy path early one morning, Mary's sharp eyes noticed something high in a tree. It was a man dressed all in brown. He was staring out over the camp.

He hadn't seen Mary, so she went for a closer look. She moved up the hill from tree to tree. She was careful to walk only on the bare patches that matched her brown cloak.

The man had a telescope. He was staring through the telescope and writing things down. He looked well fed and warmly dressed. Mary was sure he didn't come from Valley Forge. "A British spy!" she thought.

Quietly Mary slipped away. When she reached the icy path again, she slipped and fell. The man heard her. He looked down the hill. Then he turned away. Why should he worry about a little girl?

Mary hurried back to camp. She told an officer that she had seen a British spy. The officer at Valley Forge sent four soldiers back with Mary. The man was too busy spying on the camp to see them making their way up the hill. The soldiers made Mary hide behind a rock while they went to catch the spy.

Mary became a hero. The officers in camp all raised their hats when Mary walked by. The soldiers saluted her. Someone even heard General Washington say, "If I had more soldiers like Mary McDonald, this war would be over."

This made-up story is based on fact. General Washington's army did camp at Valley Forge in the winter of 1777–1778. The army was short of food and clothes. Martha Washington spent much of the winter at the camp. She and the other women took food to the soldiers. They fixed clothes. They took care of the sick. The women at the camp tried to help the soldiers as much as they could.

1. What did Mary do to help her country?

2. Which thing could Mary do that grown-ups could not? Why?

3. How did Mary resolve the problem after she saw the spy?

4. How did you feel when Mary slipped and fell?

5. Where in the story did you know how the soldiers felt about Mary after she had helped to catch the spy?

Think and Write

This story takes place in the winter. Think about how the story might have been different if it had taken place in the summer. Write about what things might have changed.

This story is from the book The Wonderful Wizard of Oz. *Read to find out about some of the characters Dorothy meets as she tries to find the Wizard.*

from The Wonderful Wizard of Oz

by L. Frank Baum

Dorothy and her dog, Toto, are in the Land of Oz. Dorothy wants very much to get back home to Kansas. She and Toto are looking for the Wonderful Wizard of Oz. She thinks he will help them.

Dorothy knows that the Wizard of Oz lives in the Emerald City. She is on her way there when she meets the Scarecrow.

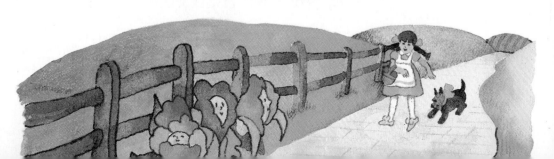

Dorothy was surprised to see one of the Scarecrow's eyes slowly wink at her.

"Good day," said the Scarecrow, in a low voice.

"Did you speak?" asked the girl.

"Certainly," replied the Scarecrow. "How do you do?"

"I'm pretty well, thank you," said Dorothy, politely. "How do you do?"

"I'm not feeling well," said the Scarecrow, with a smile. "It is very tiring being perched up here night and day to scare away crows."

"Can't you get down?" asked Dorothy.

"No. I am stuck on this pole. If you will please take me off the pole, I shall be thankful."

Dorothy reached up both arms and lifted the Scarecrow off the pole. Because he was stuffed with straw, the Scarecrow was quite light.

"Thank you very much," said the Scarecrow, when he had been set down on the ground. "I feel like a new man."

Dorothy was puzzled at this. It was strange to hear a stuffed man speak, and to see him try to stand straight.

"Who are you?" asked the Scarecrow, when he had stretched himself. "Where are you going?"

"My name is Dorothy," said the girl. "I am going to the Emerald City to ask the great Oz to send me back to Kansas."

"Where is the Emerald City?" he asked. "Who is Oz?"

"Why, don't you know?" she replied in surprise.

"No, indeed. I don't know anything. You see, I am stuffed. I have no brains at all," he replied sadly.

"Oh," said Dorothy. "I'm so very sorry for you."

"Do you think," he asked, "that if I go to the Emerald City with you, the great Oz would give me some brains?"

"I cannot tell," she said, "but you may come with me, if you like. If Oz will not give you any brains, you will be no worse off than you are now."

"No worse, that is true," said the Scarecrow. "You see," he continued, "I don't mind my legs and arms and body being stuffed, because I can't get hurt. If anyone walks on my toes or sticks a pin into me, it doesn't matter. I can't feel it. I do not want people to call me a fool, though. If my head stays stuffed with straw, instead of with brains as yours is, how am I ever to know anything?"

"I understand how you feel," said Dorothy, who was really sorry for him. "If you will come with me, I'll ask Oz to do all he can for you."

"Thank you," said the Scarecrow.

They walked back to the road. Dorothy helped him over the fence. They started along the yellow brick road to the Emerald City.

Toto, Dorothy's little dog, did not like the Scarecrow at first. He smelled around the stuffed Scarecrow and growled at him.

"Don't mind Toto," said Dorothy to
her new friend. "He never bites."

"Oh, I'm not afraid," replied the
Scarecrow. "He can't hurt the straw. Do
let me carry that basket for you. I shall
not mind it, for I can't get tired. I'll tell
you a secret," he continued, as they
walked along. "There is only one thing
in the world I am afraid of."

"What is that?" asked Dorothy. "Is it
the farmer who made you?"

"No," answered the Scarecrow. "It's a
lighted match."

Dorothy and the Scarecrow continued on their journey to the Emerald City and the Wizard of Oz. On the way they met the Tin Woodman and the Cowardly Lion.

The Tin Woodman and the Cowardly Lion wanted to see the Wonderful Wizard of Oz, too. The Tin Woodman wanted Oz to give him a heart. The Cowardly Lion wanted Oz to give him courage.

They had many adventures on the way to the Emerald City. Now they are close to it. All they must do is find the yellow brick road in the Land of Oz again. It will take them to the Emerald City, where the great Oz lives.

It was not long before Dorothy and
her friends came to the yellow brick
road. Soon they began to see fences and
houses. They were all painted green. All
the people were dressed in green clothes.
No one came near them because everyone
was afraid of the Cowardly Lion.

"This must be the Land of Oz," said
Dorothy. "We must be getting near the
Emerald City."

"Yes," said the Scarecrow. "The people
do not seem very friendly, though. I am
afraid we will not find a place to stay
for the night."

"I should like something to eat," said
Dorothy. "I'm sure Toto is hungry, too.
Let's stop at the next house and talk to
the people."

When they came to a farm house,
Dorothy walked right up to the door and
knocked. A woman opened the door just
far enough to look out and said, "What
do you want, child? Why is that lion
with you?"

"We wish to spend the night with
you, if we may," said Dorothy. "The lion
is my friend. He would not hurt you for
the world."

"Is he tame?" asked the woman,
opening the door a little wider.

"Oh, yes," said the girl. "He is a great
coward, too. He will be more afraid of
you than you are of him."

"Well," said the woman, after thinking it over and taking another look at the Cowardly Lion. "If that is so, you may come in, and I will give you something to eat and a place to sleep."

They all went into the house. Inside there were two children and a man. The man asked, "Where are you all going?"

"We are going to the Emerald City," said Dorothy. "We are going to see the Great Oz."

"Oh!" said the man. "Are you sure that Oz will see you?"

"Why not?" asked Dorothy.

"It is said that he never lets anyone near. I have been to the Emerald City many times. It is a beautiful and wonderful place, but I've never seen the Great Oz. I don't know anyone who has."

"Does he never go out?" asked the Scarecrow.

"That is hard to tell," said the man. "You see, Oz is a great Wizard. He can take any shape he wants. Some say he looks like a bird. Some say he looks like an elephant. Some say he looks like a cat. Who the real Oz is, when he is in his own shape, no one can tell."

"That is very strange," said Dorothy. "We must try, in some way, to see him, or we shall have made our journey for nothing."

"Why do you wish to see Oz?" asked the man.

"I want him to give me some brains," said the Scarecrow.

"Oh, Oz could do that," said the man. "He has more brains than he needs."

"I want him to give me a heart," said the Tin Woodman.

"That will not trouble him," said the man. "Oz has a large number of hearts, of all sizes and shapes."

"I want him to give me courage," said the Cowardly Lion.

"Oz keeps a great pot of courage in his room," said the man. "He will be glad to give you some."

"I want him to send me back to Kansas," said Dorothy.

"Where is Kansas?" asked the man.

"I don't know," said Dorothy, sadly. "It is my home, though. I'm sure it's somewhere."

"Well, Oz can do anything. I suppose he will find Kansas for you. First, however, you must get to see him."

The next morning, as soon as the sun was up, they started out. Soon they saw a beautiful green light in the sky just before them. "That must be the Emerald City," said Dorothy.

At the gate to the city, a man gave
them special glasses because the green of
the Emerald City might hurt their eyes.
Then he took a big gold key and opened
another gate. They all followed him
through the gate into the Emerald City.

1. What characters did Dorothy meet? Why did each one want to see Oz?

2. Why did Dorothy want to see the Wizard of Oz?

3. Part of everyone's wish comes true. Explain which part of everyone's wish came true.

4. Why doesn't anyone know what the Great Oz looks like?

5. How did you feel when Dorothy and her friends went through the gates to the city? Explain your answer.

6. When in the story did you think that the people at the farm were afraid of Dorothy and her friends?

Thinking About "Patterns"

Everything you read in "Patterns" had something to do with a pattern. A pattern, you remember, is something that is repeated over and over again.

You read fables which have been told for years and years. You read made-up stories set in the past. You read about the two grandfathers and the two squirrels, who lived their lives by a pattern.

As you read other stories, think about whether or not the characters fit a pattern. Then think about whether the stories might fit into a unit called "Patterns."

1. How are the selections "City Mouse and Country Mouse" and "City Grandfather, Country Grandfather" the same? How are they different?

2. Which is more like the squirrel in winter, the ant or the grasshopper? Why?

3. What might Peggy, in "A Needle Fights for Freedom," and Mary, in "Thanks to Mary," have asked the Wizard of Oz for? Why?

4. Which character's life in this unit had the most interesting pattern? Why do you think so?

Glossary*

The glossary is a special dictionary for this book. To find a word, use alphabetical, or ABC, order. For example, to find the word *swing* in the glossary, first look for the part of the glossary that has words beginning with the letter *s.* Then use the guide words to help you find the entry word *swing.* The glossary gives the meaning of the word as it is used in the book. Then the word is used in a sentence.

Sometimes different forms of the word follow the sentence. If a different form of the word, such as *swung,* is used in the book, then that word is used in the sentence.

Synonyms are included after some entries. This is shown as *syn.* if one synonym is given or *syns.* if more than one is given.

A blue box ■ at the end of the entry means that there is a picture to go with that word.

*Adapted entries that appear on the following pages are reprinted from *HBJ School Dictionary,* copyright © 1985 by Harcourt Brace Jovanovich, Inc. Reprinted by permission of Harcourt Brace Jovanovich, Inc.

A

able Having what it takes to do something: Will you be *able* to help me?

above Over: She could not reach the basketball net high *above* her. *syns.* over, overhead

abstraction Art that shows the idea of something without being a picture of it: That red painting is an *abstraction* of a bowl of apples. **abstractions**

adventure An unusual and exciting experience: I like to read about the *adventures* of heroes. **adventures**

alive Having life: The paper moves as if it were *alive*. *syn.* living

almost Nearly, but not quite: I have *almost* enough money.

apart Separated from: Our houses are a mile *apart*.

apple A round fruit that grows on trees: Would you like an *apple*? **apples** ■

army A group of soldiers trained for fighting: The *army* needs a lot of food. **armies** *syn.* troops

astronaut A space traveler: An *astronaut* must know about space. **astronauts** *syn.* spaceman or spacewoman ■

275

author A person who has written a book or story: The *author* signed a copy of her book for me. **authors** *syn.* writer

---

B

---

balance To put or keep in a state of evenness without falling: Adam was *balancing* a ball on one finger. **balanced, balancing**

barber A person who cuts people's hair and shaves them: Many men go to a *barber.* **barbers**

barbershop A place where people go for haircuts and shaves: Terry is getting his hair cut at Phil's *barbershop.* **barbershops**

basket **1** A container made of woven material: I keep my toys in that *basket.* *syn.* container **2** In basketball, a goal: Larry made a *basket* to win the game. **baskets**

basketball A sport in which two teams of five players try to throw a large ball through a basket: Dave is on the *basketball* team.

beneath Under: The banging came from the room *beneath* us. *syns.* below, underneath

besides Also; moreover: I have a cold; *besides,* my head hurts. *syns.* also, furthermore, moreover

boss The person in charge of workers: He wanted to be the *boss* of the program. **bosses**

bottle A container used to hold liquids: Those *bottles* hold apple juice. **bottles** ■

bring To take with oneself to a place: Sandy *brought* his dog home with him. **brought, bringing** *syn.* carry

bubble Air-filled liquid in the shape of a ball: The soap made many *bubbles.* **bubbles**

business What one does for a job or to make money: Bev is in the food *business.*

busy With a lot of things going on: Tuesday is a *busy* day. *syn.* active

C

candle A wax stick with a wick in it that burns when lit: Maggie lit two *candles.* **candles**

carnival A kind of entertainment with games and rides: Can we go to the *carnival* in town? **carnivals** *syn.* fair ■

carrot A long, thin, orange vegetable: Betsy ate a *carrot.* **carrots**

cause A person or thing that makes something happen: The rain is the *cause* of the game starting so late. **causes** *syn.* reason

certainly Surely: This is certainly the best story you have ever written. *syn.* surely

cloudy Weather in which clouds cover the sun: It's too *cloudy* for our picnic.

coatroom A room where coats, hats, boots, and the like are kept: I hung my jacket in the *coatroom.* **coatrooms** *syn.* closet

collar 1 A part of clothing that goes around the neck: The shirt's *collar* is blue. 2 A piece of leather or metal that goes around a dog's neck: My dog has a brown *collar*. **collars.**

colony A group of people ruled by another country: Massachusetts was one of the original thirteen *colonies*. **colonies** *syn.* settlement

comb A tool with teeth, used to make hair neat: Those *combs* cost a dollar. **combs**

continue To keep going on: We *continued* to work hard on our books. **continued, continuing**

copy Something made to look like something else: These are *copies* of George Washington's letter. **copies**

corner The part of a room where two walls meet: The cat was sleeping in the *corner*. **corners** *syn.* angle

cottony Like cotton: This hat is made of paper, but it feels *cottony*.

courage Bravery: The young girl showed *courage* when she helped the baby.

course Naturally (used with of): *Of course* I did my homework. *syn.* naturally

cousin The daughter or son of one's aunt or uncle: Nancy is my *cousin*. **cousins**

coward Someone who is not brave: No one wants to be a *coward*. **cowards**

crawl To move slowly and near the ground: Melanie's baby brother was *crawling* on the floor. **crawled, crawling** *syn.* creep

curtsy To bow with bent knees: Luisa tried *curtsying*. **curtsied, curtsying** ■

D
---

dainty Delicate; fine: What a *dainty* little doll! *syns.* fine, delicate

danger At risk of being hurt in some way: We are in *danger* of losing.

dangerous Not safe: That broken step is *dangerous*. *syn.* risky

decide To make up one's mind: Penny *decided* to stay home. **decided, deciding** *syn.* determine

deed A thing that is done: The boy's brave *deeds* saved the town. **deeds** *syn.* act

dinner The main meal of the day: We had fish for *dinner.*

domino A game piece marked with dots: Sara played a game with her *dominoes*. **dominoes** ■

double Two times as many, as much, or as large: I'll have a *double* order of pancakes. *syn.* twice

drawer A part of a piece of furniture that slides out and is used to keep things in: Put your clothes in the *drawer.* **drawers**

279

E

earn   To get paid for working: The girls *earn* money by cutting the grass. **earned, earning**

either   Besides; on the other hand: Max isn't short, but he isn't tall *either. syn.* besides

elbow   The joint where the arm bends: Let me see the cut on your *elbow.* **elbows** ■

elevator   A machine that carries people and things up and down in a building: Sammy took the *elevator* to the fifth floor. **elevators**

especially   More than usually: I love breakfast, and I *especially* love pancakes. *syn.* particularly

exactly   In the same way; just: Our coats were *exactly* the same. *syn.* just

excite   To stir up or to have strong feelings: Beth is *excited* about the gym meet. **excited, exciting**

excitement   The state of being excited, or stirred up: There was too much *excitement* for the baby.

exercise   **1** To use body movements to make oneself strong and healthy: We should *exercise* every day. **2** These movements: Our class does *exercises* every morning. **exercises**

expect   To know or think one knows what is coming: I *expected* Mrs. Gross to be much taller. **expected, expecting**

extra More than needed: We had some *extra* food. *syn.* spare

---

F

---

fact Used with *in:* Really or actually: I have never been there, *in fact.*

famous Known by many people: That is a *famous* book.

fiddle To play the fiddle, or violin: The man sang and the boy *fiddled.* **fiddled, fiddling** ■

fighter A person who fights against something: The police officer is a crime *fighter.* **fighters** *syn.* battler

finally At last: The end of the long day *finally* came. *syn.* lastly

floor The bottom of a room: Put the box on the *floor.* **floors**

forget To not remember: The sailor must have *forgotten* where he put the boat. **forgot, forgotten, forgetting**

freedom The state of being free: Many people have worked hard for *freedom.* *syn.* liberty

furniture Items in a house, such as beds, chairs, chests, and tables: Eric sells *furniture* in his store. ■

281

furry Covered in fur or material like fur: A *furry* robe is warm on a cold morning. *syn.* hairy

G

gather To get together or collect: Jacob is *gathering* his things now. **gathered, gathering** *syn.* collect

give To offer or hand over: We were *given* a lot of work to do. **gave, given, giving** *syn.* present

golden 1 Made of gold: Those are *golden* coins. 2 The color of gold: The sky is *golden*.

guard A person who keeps something or someone from harm: The *guard* is very strong. **guards** *syn.* keeper

guess To decide without being sure: Can you *guess* who came to visit? **guessed, guessing** *syn.* predict

guinea pig A small, furry animal that looks something like a rat: I fed the *guinea pig*. **guinea pigs** ■

H

heart The part of the body that pumps blood: The doctor listened to my *heart*. **hearts**

hero A very brave person: The woman who saved the child from the fire is a *hero*. **heroes**

hide To put something
where it cannot be seen:
Steve has *hidden* his keys.
hid, hidden, hiding *syn.*
conceal

homework Schoolwork that
is to be done at home:
Aliza did her *homework*
after supper. *syn.*
assignment

hooray A shout of
happiness or cheering for
someone or something:
Hooray, it's snowing! *syns.*
hurrah, yippee

hour Sixty minutes: Judd
will study for an *hour.*
hours

I
---

icy Covered with ice: The
sidewalk is *icy* today.
indeed In truth: This is
a great dinner, *indeed*.

information Facts about
something: This book has
information about shells.
syns. knowledge, facts

instead In place of another:
Jackie couldn't go, so Ray
went *instead*.

J
---

jacket A coat that is short:
My new *jacket* is green.
jackets *syn.* coat ■

journey A trip: Betsy went
on a *journey* to New York.
journeys *syn.* trip

K

kitchen The room where food is kept and cooked: Come into the *kitchen*. **kitchens**

kitten A cat when it is young: The *kitten* played with the string. **kittens** *syn.* kitty ■

knee The joint where the leg bends: My *knees* are bent. **knees**

knife A tool used for cutting: Please put the *knives* on the table. **knives**

knock To hit something to make it fall: Kevin *knocked* down the tent. **knocked, knocking** *syn.* hit

L

lady A woman: The *lady* wore a green dress. **ladies** *syns.* woman, ma'am

license A paper or something that shows that a person has permission to do or have something: Ruff, the dog, lost his *license* tag. **licenses** *syn.* permit

lock To hold in position: *Lock* your knees and stand straight. **locked, locking** *syn.* hold

lower To move down: Lift your arm and then *lower* it. **lowered, lowering**

M

ma'am A short form of *madam*, a polite way to address a woman: "Yes, *ma'am*, I'll help you," said Connie. *syn.* lady

machine A device that does a certain job: There is a *machine* that counts the eggs. **machines** *syns.* tool, utensil

market A place where things are sold: I got the carrots at the *market.* **markets** *syns.* store, shop ■

match **1** To be alike: The girls in the class had *matching* hats. **2** To find things that look the same: She wanted to *match* the red in the picture. **matched, matching** *syns.* imitate, copy

matter **1** The subject at hand: The *matter* we are talking about is clean water. *syn.* subject **2** Problem: What is the *matter* with Jordan? **matters** *syn.* problem

message News or information sent to someone else: I got a *message* from Uncle Hal. **messages** *syn.* note

miller A person whose job it is to make flour: The *miller* gave us the flour for the bread. **millers**

mistake An error; something wrong: Carolyn made a *mistake* on her paper. **mistakes** *syn.* error

mood A state of mind; how one feels: Sally was in a good *mood* yesterday. **moods**

motion To signal by moving: The teacher *motions* us to come in. **motioned, motioning** *syn.* signal

museum A place where people can see art and other exhibits: I love to go to science *museums.* **museums** *syn.* gallery ■

mystery A thing that isn't understood or explained: What happened to the coins is a *mystery.* **mysteries** *syns.* puzzle, riddle

---
N
---

needle A tool used to put thread through cloth for sewing: The *needle* broke, so I couldn't fix your shirt. **needles**

noise A sound: Margy heard a loud *noise.* **noises** *syn.* sound

number A label given to something to tell in which order it comes: Do *numbers* 1–5 in your workbooks. **numbers**

O
---

ocean A large body of salt water: The *oceans* are home to many fish. **oceans** *syn.* sea

oil To put oil on: She *oiled* the parts of the machine before she used it. **oiled, oiling** *syn.* grease

order Things or events put one after the other: The children do their work in *order* every day—first reading, then spelling. *syn.* pattern

P

paragraph A part of something written, usually a group of sentences: Please read the first *paragraph*. **paragraphs**

pattern A guide used in making something: Use a *pattern* to help you cut out the pieces for your kite. **patterns** *syn.* model ■

pencil A tool used for writing: Todd broke his *pencil*. **pencils**

piece 1 A part of something separated from the rest: This is a *piece* of the broken cup. 2 A part of a set: I found these *pieces* from your game. **pieces** *syns.* portion, part

pleasure Something that makes one pleased or content: Driving in our new car is a *pleasure*. **pleasures** *syns.* joy, happiness, delight

plenty Enough; a lot of: We have *plenty* of time before the game. *syn.* enough

poem Writing that is in verse, often rhyming: Chan's favorite *poem* is "Clouds." **poems**

polite Having or showing good manners: Thomas was very *polite* to his teachers. *syn.* courteous

predict To say ahead of time: We can *predict* how the story will end. **predicted, predicting** *syn.* forecast

prediction The act of predicting: Sue made a *prediction* about the story, and she was right. *syn.* guess

private Not for everybody to see or hear about: What I just told you is *private*. *syn*. secret

probably Very likely: Joe's team will *probably* win. *syn*. likely

program A plan: Our written *program* helps us become better writers. **programs** *syn*. plan

puddle A pool of water or other liquid: Don't step in the *puddles*. **puddles**

puffy Airy and soft: The quilt was *puffy* and warm. *syn*. fluffy

punch A fruit drink: She filled the glasses with *punch* for the party.

purpose Reason: My *purpose* for reading this story is to find out how Jenny solves the mystery. **purposes** *syn*. reason

puzzle A toy in which parts are put together: My sister played with her new *puzzle*. **puzzles** ■

R
---

recess A short time out from work, especially at school: James and Nate played ball at *recess*.

reply To answer: "Thank you," *replied* Seth. **replied, replying** *syns*. answer, respond

retire To give up a job, usually because one is getting older: Ms. Brown *retired* from her job as a bus driver. **retired, retiring**

return To come back: I *returned* home late.
returned, returning

robber A person who steals: The *robber* took Tommy's watch. **robbers** *syns.* burglar, thief

robbery The stealing of something that belongs to another: There's a *robbery* going on at the bank! **robberies** *syn.* burglary

robot A machine that can do jobs that people usually do: The *robot* in the factory puts the bicycles together. **robots** ■

rocky Filled with rocks: The beach here is very *rocky*. *syn.* stony

runner Someone who runs for sport or exercise: The *runner* came by a minute ago. **runners** *syn.* jogger

---

S

salute To raise or move the hand in a certain way in greeting: The soldier *saluted* the general. **saluted, saluting** *syn.* greet

sandwich Two pieces of bread with a food filling between them: I'll have a cheese *sandwich*. **sandwiches** ■

schoolmaster The head of a school: Our *schoolmaster* is kind. **schoolmasters** *syn.* principal

289

scold To talk sharply to someone: He was *scolding* her for making a hole in his kite. **scolded, scolding**

season A certain time of the year: Fall is the *season* for picking apples. **seasons**

secret Something private that is not told: The party is a *secret.* **secrets**

sequence A number of things following each other: The *sequence* of the story was easy to follow.

settle To put in place: We are *settled* in our new house. **settled, settling**

seventeen Ten plus seven, written as 17: There are *seventeen* girls in our class.

seventy Sixty plus ten, written as 70: There are *seventy* houses on our street.

shiny Gleaming brightly: The cat had *shiny* black fur. *syns.* glossy, polished

shirt A piece of clothing worn over the chest, back, and arms: My *shirt* is blue. **shirts** *syns.* top, blouse ■

shiver To shake with fear or cold: Anita *shivered* when she walked into the cold room. **shivered, shivering** *syns.* tremble, quake, shudder

soldier A person in the army: The *soldiers* led the parade. **soldiers** *syn.* serviceman, servicewoman

solve To figure out: Annie *solved* the problem. **solved, solving**

somehow In a way one is not sure about: I *somehow* got my work done on time.

sorry Feeling bad about something: I'm *sorry* I ran over your bike.

spacecraft A spaceship or vehicle: The *spacecraft* was on its way to Mars. **spacecrafts** *syn.* spaceship

squirrel A small animal with a bushy tail: The gray *squirrel* is looking for food. **squirrels** ■

sticky Like glue: Paste makes your hands *sticky*.

strange Odd: That was a strange *answer* Melissa gave. *syns.* odd, queer

straw Dried grasses: We put down *straw* for the horses to sleep on. *syn.* hay

study To try to know or learn: Joe *studied* his spelling words. **studied, studying**

sure Certainly: "I *sure* am hungry," said the man on the horse. *syns.* certainly, definitely

---
T
---

telephone A machine that allows people to talk to each other over wires: Please get in touch with me by *telephone*. **telephones** *syn.* phone

telescope An instrument that makes faraway things look bigger or nearer: We could see the valleys of the moon through the *telescope*. **telescopes**

terrible Awful: We had a *terrible* time finding you. *syn.* awful

thankful Happy about something good: They were *thankful* when the truck finally brought their furniture. *syns.* pleased, grateful

thirteen Ten plus three, written as 13: There are *thirteen* apples in the bowl.

tickle Touch in a way that makes one laugh or twitch: Feathers make my skin *tickle*. **tickled, tickling**

tiptoe To walk quietly, as if walking on the tips of one's toes: Marvin *tiptoed* into his brother's room. **tiptoed, tiptoeing**

tomorrow The day after this day: I forgot the money, so I'll bring it *tomorrow*.

tonight This night: The celebration will start *tonight*.

toward In the direction of: Vanessa pointed *toward* the door.

tractor A strong farm vehicle used to pull plows and other tools: Mary learned to drive a *tractor*. **tractors** ■

trouble A problem; difficulty: Sam had *trouble* doing his homework. *syns.* problem, difficulty

U

unfriendly Not acting in a friendly way: The dog was *unfriendly*, so I didn't go near it.

unhappy Sad; not satisfied: Valerie was *unhappy* about her spelling test mark. *syn.* sad

---
V
---

valley A low spot between hills or mountains: The hills and *valleys* are beautiful. **valleys**

vapor Gas: Water turns to *vapor* as it gets hotter. *syns.* gas, cloud

village A very small town: The people go to the *village* to buy food. **villages**

W
---

wagon A small, wheeled vehicle that is moved by pulling: The little boy rode in the *wagon*. **wagons** *syn.* cart

wash To clean, usually with soap and water: Carmen, *wash* your face. **washed, washing** *syn.* launder

whisker A hair that sticks out of the side of some animals' faces: The cat washed its *whiskers*. **whiskers** ■

windowsill The little shelf across the bottom of a window: Put the plant on the *windowsill*. **windowsills**

workbook A book in which students do schoolwork: Take out your reading *workbooks*. **workbooks**

293

Word List

The following words are introduced in this book. Each is listed beside the number of the page on which it first appears.

Backyard Basketball Superstar
(6–13)

6 basketball
   season
   Flyers
   tomorrow
7 basket
8 sure

"E" Is for Exercise
(16–21)

16 exercising
18 numbers
19 floor
    lock
    lower
    knees
    elbows

Sequence
(22–23)

22 sequence
    order

Today Was a Terrible Day
(24–31)

24 terrible
    pencil

    crawling
25 homework
    forgotten
    besides
    tiptoed
    coatroom
    sandwich
26 mistake
    workbook
    almost
27 finally
    carrot
28 guess
    somehow
    knocked
    windowsill

Predict Outcomes
(32–33)

32 predict
    probably
33 strange
    prediction

The Balancing Girl
(34–43)

34 carnival
    balancing
35 private
    corner
    recess

36 sorry
37 trouble
38 dominoes
40 noise
42 hooray

What Can You Do with Dominoes?
(46–51)

46 pieces
47 double
48 matching

My Grandpa Retired Today
(52–59)

52 retired
    barbershop
53 oiled
    barber
    wash
    combs
    saluted
    bottles

Jasper and the Hero Business
(66–75)

66 hero